JAMAICA

POCKET GUIDE

ARTS & CULTURE
Space disco featuring
Music
DIAMANT
Restaurant
100 m
BROOKLAWN
JOE'S BURGERS
Restaurant
100 m
A TO Z INFO
SHOPPIN
ATE BRIDGE
100 m
MAP
SHARE
LIKE
Sailing under the Golden Gate Bridge today, it is interesting to consider that engineers once thought it impossible to span the Golden Gate Strait at this point, because of the depth of the water (318ft/97 meters, at its deepest point) and the power ful tidal rush.
The city authorized studies for a bridge in 1917, but it was 1933 before the first shovel turned under the gaze of master engineer Joseph B. Strauss (no relation to the famous waltz composer). Four years later the bridge opened, at a cost of $35 million and the lives of 11 construction workers. Today the bridge
INSIGHT GUIDES
SPAIN
INTRODUCTION
EXPLORE
$8.00
ORIDA
This new edition of Insight Guide Florida is a comprehensive, full-colour travel guide packed with inspiration and information. It includes engrossing features on everything from colonial Turf Wars and ...
$8.00
FRANCE
This brand new edition Insight Guide to France features outstanding full-colour photography, with this edition containing over 250 brand new photographs, alongside illuminating explorations of all the places to go ...
$8.00
ST LUCIA Pocket Guide
$8.00

Walking Eye
mobile app

Discover the world's best destinations with the Insight Guides Walking Eye app, available to download for free in the App Store and Google Play.

The container app provides easy access to fantastic free content on events and activities taking place in your current location or chosen destination, with the possibility of booking, as well as the regularly-updated Insight Guides travel blog: Inspire Me. In addition, you can purchase curated, premium destination guides through the app, which feature local highlights, hotel, bar, restaurant and shopping listings, an A to Z of practical information and more. Or purchase and download Insight Guides eBooks straight to your device.

Download on the App Store

GET IT ON Google Play

TOP 10 ATTRACTIONS

ROSE HALL GREAT HOUSE

Some believe that this landmark property is haunted. See page 34.

YS FALLS

Fun for all at this tiered waterfall fringed by mature forest. See page 76.

SEVEN MILE BEACH

This stretch of fine sand is considered one of the best beaches in the Caribbean. See page 80.

BLUE MOUNTAINS

Explore this magnificent mountain range on a guided walk. See page 60.

RUNAWAY BAY

One of the most popular resorts on the north coast. See page 40.

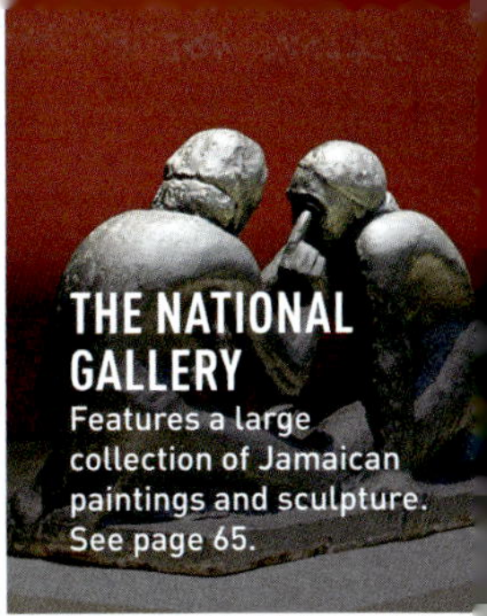

THE NATIONAL GALLERY

Features a large collection of Jamaican paintings and sculpture. See page 65.

BLACK RIVER

Home to a variety of birds, fish and crocodiles. See page 76.

BOB MARLEY MUSEUM

A fascinating insight into the life and work of the reggae icon. See page 68.

TREASURE BEACH

An ideal place for a relaxing getaway on the south coast. See page 78.

DUNN'S RIVER FALLS

No visit to Jamaica is complete without a walk up these famous falls. See page 45.

A PERFECT DAY

7.00am

Early swim

Start the day with a refreshing swim on Seven Mile Beach. You'll have the place to yourself apart from a few joggers and early birds, and the sea will be blissfully calm.

8.00am

Breakfast/ lighthouse

Tuck into a full Jamaican breakfast, either at your hotel or at Just Natural restaurant at West End. Then stroll to the Victorian Lighthouse, where you get a great view out to sea and along the cliffs.

10.00am

Craft market

Back to Seven Mile Beach by taxi and wander around the craft stalls for a bargain. Pick up some snacks for later – fresh fruit from the women on the beach and delicious patties from Niah's Patties.

11.00am

Taxi tour

Find a reputable taxi driver outside your hotel and agree a rate for a tour of the south coast. Head for Bluefields Bay, via Savanna la Mar.

11.30am

Blue Hole

Spend time at the Blue Hole, jumping 7.5m (25ft) into the water or sunbathing around the spring-fed pool. Call in at the Peter Tosh Mausoleum at Belmont, a shrine to the superstar reggae musician.

IN NEGRIL

5.30pm

Take a sunset cruise

Sail off into the sunset with a rum punch and watch the last flickering rays of the day. You'll be taken to the rocky cliffs at West End, before stopping off at Rick's Café to see intrepid young cliff-jumpers fling themselves off the rocks.

10.00pm

Night fever

Head for The Jungle, the iconic club where you can work up a sweat on one of the four dance floors. Security is tight and the music carries on until the last guest staggers out.

2.30pm

Black River

Take a boat tour a few miles up the longest river in Jamaica and into the Great Morass, the swamp where the crocodiles live, and fit in a spot of birdwatching before returning to Negril.

7.30pm

Romantic dinner

Enjoy a romantic candlelit meal at Ivan's Bar & Restaurant at Catcha Falling Star Hotel, nestled on top of Negril's scenic cliffs. Take in the beautiful view while sipping a cocktail or two.

CONTENTS

INTRODUCTION 10

A BRIEF HISTORY 15

WHERE TO GO 27

Montego Bay 28
Downtown 29, The Beaches 30, South of the Bay 32

East on the Coast Road 34
Great Houses 34, Falmouth 36, Cockpit Country 38, Discovery Bay and Runaway Bay 39, St Ann's Bay 41

Ocho Rios to Annotto Bay 42
Dunn's River Falls 45, Rivers and Plantations 45, Firefly and Annotto Bay 47

Port Antonio and the East 51
Port Antonio 52, West of Port Antonio 54, East of Port Antonio 56, Jamaica's Eastern Tip 57, The Blue Mountains 60

Kingston and Environs 63
Downtown 64, New Kingston 67, Port Royal 69

Central Highlands and the South 71
Spanish Town 72, Mandeville 74, Black River 76, Treasure Beach 77

Negril and the West 79
Negril 79, To the South 83

WHAT TO DO 85

Sports and Outdoor Activities 85
Nightlife and Entertainment 93
Shopping 94
Children's Jamaica 97

EATING OUT 100

A–Z TRAVEL TIPS 114

RECOMMENDED HOTELS 132

INDEX 142

FEATURES

Rastafari Movement 13
The Lady Pirates 18
Marcus Garvey – A National Hero 23
Historical Landmarks 25
'Daddy' Samuel Sharpe 29
Duppies and Obeah 38
Jamaica's Best Beaches 50
Jamaica's 'Higglers' 64
Jamaica's Predatory Pest 69
Aloe Vera 80
Jamaica's Top Dive Sites 87
Festivals and Events 99

INTRODUCTION

The island of Jamaica amazed Christopher Columbus when he visited in 1494 on his second journey to the West Indies. He described it as the 'fairest island' and marvelled at the mountains that 'touched the sky'. Today's visitors will be equally charmed by the warm sunshine, beautiful beaches, rivers and streams that gush from ravines, lush tropical scenery and majestic mountains, as well as the vibrant grassroots culture.

LANDSCAPE AND VEGETATION

The third-largest island in the Caribbean, just south of Cuba, Jamaica is 235km (146 miles) in length and 82km (51 miles) across at its widest point. The island is aligned almost east-to-west in the water so that sunrise wakes the eastern tip, proceeds to caress the length of the island, and kisses the western tip 'good night'. Geographically it is extremely diverse, with a central backbone of high mountains blanketed with a mixture of wet limestone forests and plantations of pine and native hardwood trees, such as mahoe and cedar. These are surrounded by areas of limestone formations, scrub and grassland, coral cliffs and fine sand beaches. Fresh water springs and tropical storms feed 120 rivers and some of the most celebrated waterfalls and cascades on earth.

On land, there is a wealth of animal and bird life. Rare species of butterflies and delicate hummingbirds take to the air, and crocodiles and a few manatees still live in and around large tracts of mangrove swamp in the south.

The island is surrounded by coral reefs, which provide shelter for sea creatures and endless hours of recreation for divers and snorkellers.

Temperatures generally vary only a few degrees around 27°C (80°F), although the heat is tempered by the nearly continuous trade winds that blow across the Atlantic. In the mountains and hills of the interior, the temperature drops with altitude to as low as 3°C (37°F) on the mist-covered Blue Mountain Peak, the island's highest point at 2,256m (7,402ft).

Bananas: a cash crop

Much of the land is extremely fertile and produces a range of tropical fruit and vegetable crops such as yams, sweet potatoes and juicy mangoes, providing ample food for the people, as well as cash crops such as bananas, sugar and coffee. Four hundred years ago these crops brought British colonists to rule the land and African slaves to work it, forever changing the landscape and the population.

NATIONAL IDENTITY

Today's Jamaicans are a mixture of African and English people, with Spanish, Indian and a smattering of Portuguese, Jews, Chinese, Welsh and Irish. The cultures have melded together, giving rise to a fascinating national identity.

Since gaining independence in 1962, the black majority has worked to create a country based on confidence from within, working on a principle of pride in oneself and in one's roots.

Store owner in Ocho Rios

This is so important for the future of the country that the national motto is 'Out of many – one people'.

Like most of the Caribbean islands, Jamaica was originally inhabited by Amerindians who had migrated from South America. The arrival of the Spanish at the end of the 15th century had a cataclysmic effect. Nowadays there is little evidence of the Castilian colonists, nor of the Amerindians they wiped out with their brutal slavery and European diseases – 160 years of Spanish rule have been blotted out by 307 years as a British colony.

Vestiges of the British colonial legacy can still be found, not least in the fact that English is Jamaica's official language: the popularity of cricket is another example. The 13 regional parishes and numerous towns were originally named after British settlements. You can find Manchester, Sheffield and Cambridge in Jamaica, to name but three. However, these British influences have, even from the earliest days of colonial rule, always been tempered and moulded to the Jamaican style. Jamaica has always had a second 'unofficial' language developed from the early days of slavery. This creole, a mixture of English, African and Spanish words and phrases, is still evolving and is often indecipherable to the outsider. Next to town names derived from Spain and England, you'll also find names such as 'Wait Awhile' and 'Fruitful Vale', derived from the land and lifestyle of Jamaica.

The influence of the United States is now much stronger than that of Britain. Many Jamaicans head to the States for further education, and American economic influence is strong: the US dollar is accepted (and most times even preferred) as readily as the Jamaican dollar to pay for goods.

However, Jamaica still revels in its own identity, which is now internationally recognised through such influential cultural products as the Rastafari movement and reggae music. The Rastafari movement originated in Jamaica in the 1930s and is still predominantly found here. Jamaican music – ska and, especially, reggae – has, since the 1970s, been exported and enjoyed around the world. The strong beat and earthy lyrics seem to symbolise and celebrate the character of this young

RASTAFARI MOVEMENT

One of the most popular images of Jamaica is that of the Rasta. His mane of dreadlocks and colourful 'tam' hat are instantly recognisable worldwide. Rastafari live by a series of strict rules. They are nonviolent and do not eat meat. Rastas use marijuana as an integral part of their religious experience and do not cut their hair, fearing the same loss of spiritual and physical strength that the biblical Samson experienced.

Members of the Rastafari sect believe themselves to be one of the tribes of Israel, viewing the modern world as 'Babylon', synonymous with evil, and they seek peace with God, whom they believe is in all beings. Their spiritual leader is Haile Selassie, the late emperor of Ethiopia, who was God's messenger on earth – the 'Lion of Judah'.

Jamaican handshake

The traditional Jamaican handshake – with clenched fists meeting first vertically then horizontally, after which the thumbs touch briefly – signals a parting of mutual understanding and respect.

and lively country. The country's latest accolade is down to Marlon James, the first Jamaican author to win the Man Booker Prize. His novel *A Brief History of Seven Killings* tells the fictional history of the attempted murder of Bob Marley in 1976. It won the Man Booker in 2015.

TOURIST ATTRACTIONS

Since independence in 1962, tourism has become a major employer and source of income and the island is renowned as one of the top destinations in the Caribbean. While some of the hotels that attracted writers and film stars in the 1950s are still going strong as luxury hideaways, Jamaica has also pioneered the all-inclusive resort catering for the mass market. The best beaches are now home to some fine hotels and large resorts.

It is tempting, and possible, to spend your entire holiday in a resort. Yet to do this is to miss the very essence of what the island is all about. Learn how to do the Jamaican handshake. Taste authentic Caribbean dishes such as *ackee* and saltfish (Jamaica's national dish), and aromatic hot jerk pork cooked in a pit barbecue. Savour a freshly ground cup of Blue Mountain coffee or enjoy a fine, aged Jamaican rum. Hear the dance hall and reggae music booming from a hundred cranked-up car stereos or the chorus of tiny tree frogs that begins as evening descends. Jamaica is an island with a strong personality that doesn't simply wait in the wings. It comes out to meet you.

A BRIEF HISTORY

The earliest signs of people on Jamaica are the remains of the Taino, Amerindians descending from Arawak-speaking people who migrated from the north coast of South America. They travelled to various Caribbean islands along the entire Antillean chain, arriving in Jamaica at the beginning of the 8th century.

The Tainos left an important legacy of rock paintings and carvings in places such as Runaway Caves near Discovery Bay, and shards of pottery found at their settlements near Sevilla la Nueva and Spanish Town have added a little to our knowledge about them. Over 200 Taino sites have been identified, and it is said that when the Spanish arrived in Jamaica there were approximately 100,000 Tainos living on the island. They called Jamaica *Xaymaca* ('land of wood and water').

COLUMBUS AND THE ARRIVAL OF EUROPEANS

Christopher Columbus first arrived in Jamaica on 5 May 1494. He stayed for only a few days but on his fourth voyage he spent a year stranded here in 1502–3, while his ships were being repaired. However, the island was not settled by the Spanish

Statue of Christopher Columbus, St Ann's Bay

until 1509. The year before, Columbus's son Diego had been appointed Governor of the Indies by the Spanish monarchy and he made Juan de Esquivel Governor of Jamaica.

In 1510, Esquivel created a base called Sevilla la Nueva near St Ann's Bay, from which he hoped to colonise the rest of the island. The Spanish immediately began subjugating the native Arawak-speaking population, most of whom died under the yoke of oppression and of diseases carried by the Europeans.

The site of Sevilla la Nueva proved unhealthy and mosquito-ridden, and in 1534 the Spanish founded Villa de la Vega, today known as Spanish Town. Pig breeding was the main occupation of these early settlers, but they also planted sugar cane and other crops that required large numbers of labourers. The number of Taino had already fallen dramatically, so the Spanish began to import enslaved people from Africa to work the land; the first Africans arrived in 1517.

The island was never fully exploited by the Spanish. They were much more interested in the gold and other treasures to be found in South America. However, they had to protect the shipping lanes in order to get their treasure home, and this meant keeping hold of as much of the Caribbean (or the 'Spanish Main', as it was then known) as possible. They fortified the more strategic islands, but Jamaica was deemed less important than Cuba or Puerto Rico and, consequently, was poorly protected.

BRITISH RULE

In 1654 Oliver Cromwell, Lord Protector of England, dispatched a British fleet to the Caribbean to break the stranglehold of the Spanish. They were repulsed at Hispaniola by a strong Spanish force and decided to take Jamaica as a consolation prize. They sailed into what is now Kingston Bay in May 1655 and sent an ultimatum to the capital. The small Spanish force considered its position and decided to retreat, heading to the north coast and sailing to Cuba. Before they left, they freed their slaves, who fled into the interior of the island.

The British flag flies in Kingston

The Spanish attempted to retake the island in 1658 at the Battle of Rio Bueno but were defeated. Other European powers also began to put pressure on the defending forces and British naval power in the area was badly stretched. Sir Thomas Modyford, the Governor of Jamaica, offered a deal to pirate ships already well established in the area: if the pirates protected British assets, then they were free to harass enemy shipping with impunity. They agreed, and Modyford authorised the pirates to act in the name of the British Crown.

These 'privateers' were welcomed at Port Royal, the English settlement on the southern tip of Kingston harbour, and it quickly developed a reputation as the wickedest city in the world. Plunder was now legitimate business and the city was awash with money and booty from the numerous pirate raids. There was little evidence of religion or of the rule of law. Henry Morgan was chief among the pirate leaders. He and his followers conducted a successful series of bloody raids on Spanish settlements in the Caribbean, culminating in the sacking of Panama, the major city of the Spanish Main.

In 1670 the Spanish officially ceded Jamaica to Britain as part of the Treaty of Madrid, and the British began a systematic process of settlement, offering land to prospective settlers. They rescinded their agreement with the privateers and began to evict them from Port Royal.

Henry Morgan was offered the post of Lieutenant Governor of the island and charged with driving out his former cohorts. The erstwhile pirate thus became a policeman during the last years of his life. Morgan died in 1688 before his task was complete, but nature finished what he had started: Jamaica suffered a powerful earthquake in 1692, and Port Royal sank into the sea, taking with it many of the treasures stolen from the Spanish.

PLANTATIONS AND SLAVERY

As the 18th century began, the trade in sugar cane and spices was becoming profitable. Plantation work was labour intensive, but there were few labourers on the island. The decision was made to import a workforce from West Africa, resulting in some 600,000 enslaved Africans being transported to Jamaica over the next few decades. One in five slaves died en route and many more died of

THE LADY PIRATES

The pirates who sailed the Caribbean were joined by two women, Mary Read and Anne Bonney, who were said to be as ruthless as their compatriots. They dressed in men's clothing and committed unspeakable atrocities in the name of profit. Captured by the British authorities, they were found guilty of piracy and sentenced to death, but both pleaded 'the belly'. Judges would not kill an unborn child, so both sentences were commuted to life in jail. Mary Read and her young child died of fever only a few months later, but there is no record of what happened to Anne Bonney. Her life after the trial is a mystery.

disease once on the island. On the back of this cruel system, Jamaica gradually became the biggest sugar producer in the world and a very wealthy island indeed.

Henry Morgan

Thirteen administrative parishes were created, forming the basis of government that we still see today. The Governor commissioned a representative (or custos) in each parish. Powerful land-owning families organised an Assembly to run the everyday affairs of the island, but many landowners continued to live in Britain, where they exerted tremendous influence in Parliament to protect their Jamaican interests.

Even in these early days there were slaves who fought against the tyranny of the system. The African slaves whom the Spanish had released after 1655 were known as Maroons, from the Spanish word *cimarrón* (which means 'wild' or 'untamed'). They made their settlements in the hills away from the British but began to attack colonists in a series of raids known as The First Maroon War. British forces suffered constant harassment at their hands and even named a part of the island 'The Land of Look Behind' in recognition of the surprise attacks they suffered. Eventually the British forced the Maroons into more isolated and remote pockets of land.

This war of attrition ended in 1739, when an agreement was reached between the two sides. The Maroons were allowed self-rule in designated areas in return for not helping escaped slaves. This agreement is at the root of Maroon self-government today. The plantation slaves also began organising revolts (the first in 1760), but their situation remained the same and they endured cruel and inhumane treatment.

During the American War of Independence, Jamaica came under threat again from other European powers, which saw Britain's problem to the north as a chance to capture its colonies in the Caribbean. Some islands were taken by the French, but Admiral Rodney saved Jamaica by defeating the French fleet at the Battle of Les Saintes in 1782. Jamaica thereafter became an island of strategic importance for the British, who based a large naval fleet at Fort Charles in Port Royal.

EMANCIPATION

The French Revolution in 1789 sent ripples of discontent through the Caribbean. The French peasants' cry for freedom prompted another Maroon War on Jamaica, after which many Maroons were deported to Nova Scotia. There was, however, a growing abolition movement in Britain. In 1807 Parliament made the trade in slaves illegal, but the powerful sugar lobby ensured that slavery continued on the plantations. The enslaved people were angry and dispirited. Nonconformist churches encouraged the slaves to stand up and take action against injustice. Their intervention guaranteed the popularity of these Christian denominations; Baptist and Adventist churches are still as strong today as in the early 1800s.

The momentum for change was growing, and in 1831 a

Rodney's riches

Following his decisive victory at the Battle of Les Saintes in 1782, Admiral George Rodney was honoured by the Crown with a barony and a pension of £2,000 a year.

lay preacher named 'Daddy' Sam Sharpe led a revolt of 20,000 slaves at Montego Bay. After a campaign of destruction, the authorities assured them that slavery would be abolished. Sharpe and approximately 1,000 other slaves surrendered peacefully, only to be rounded up and publicly executed. This news was met with revulsion in Britain and eventually led to full freedom in 1838.

Celebrating freedom

Unfortunately, being 'free' solved none of the problems suffered by the population. There was no economic infrastructure outside the plantation system, and power remained in the hands of a small minority of white and mixed-race individuals. Meanwhile, Asian labourers took up the work previously carried out by the enslaved Africans; their descendants can still be found on the island, particularly around Little London in the west. As a further blow to the economy, the British Parliament passed the Sugar Equalisation Act in 1846 as part of a new free-trade policy. Jamaica's protected market was effectively gone.

In October 1865 at Morant Bay, there was another uprising, led by Baptist minister Paul Bogle and George Gordon, a mixed-heritage landowner. It brought savage retribution from the authorities, and both leaders were executed, but it prompted the dissolution of the Jamaica Assembly, which was dominated by plantation owners. The island became a Crown Colony ruled directly from

Marcus Garvey

London, and over the next few years there were several reforms to its political and social systems.

As the sugar trade declined in importance, economic disaster loomed. Fortuitously, another crop found favour with the industrial world: Jamaica became the island of bananas. The first consignments were exported in 1866 and, within a few years, thousands of tons were being shipped to markets in the US and Britain. The boats carrying the banana crops also fostered a fledgling tourist trade. The first visitors arrived as passengers on them, spending time around Port Antonio.

Still there was little change in conditions for the black majority, who had no economic or political power. The worldwide depression of the 1930s brought a new wave of demonstrations in Jamaica, and a number of individuals emerged to lead the people and pave the way for nationhood: Marcus Garvey called for self-reliance; in 1938, Norman W. Manley founded the People's National Party (PNP), which found allies in the Jamaica Trades Union Congress and the National Workers Union; Manley's cousin, Sir Alexander Bustamante, formed the Industrial Trade Union and later (1944) the Jamaica Labour Party (JLP). Together, these organisations fought for local rule, which in 1944 resulted in universal voting rights for adults. At the same time, the early years of World War II brought American tourists who were no longer able to travel to Europe on holiday. Jamaica's popularity as a tourist destination was now undeniable.

INDEPENDENCE AND DEMOCRATIC RULE

In the post-war period there continued to be constitutional changes, including self-government for Jamaica in 1959. Britain hoped to create a Federation of Caribbean Islands in the region. Jamaica joined the West Indies Federation in 1958 but withdrew in 1961 following a national referendum.

Since independence in 1962, the political culture of Jamaica, which started out with such confidence and optimism, has been fraught with problems. Violence and corruption have been constant factors in the political process. From 1962 until 1972, the JLP held power. The party's broad aims were to support capitalist policies and to continue close ties with Britain and the rest of the Commonwealth.

MARCUS GARVEY – A NATIONAL HERO

Born in St Ann's Bay in 1887, Marcus Mosiah Garvey made his mark as a nationalist, instigating a 'back to Africa' movement. Garvey founded the Universal Negro Improvement Association (UNIA), advocating black unity and pride, and in 1916 he set up a UNIA office in New York. His political activities included the establishment of the Black Star Line steamship company and a newspaper, *The Negro World*, which became a forum for labour grievances. In 1925 Garvey was imprisoned for fraud on what are now considered false charges and later deported from the US. He died in obscurity in London in 1940, but after independence his remains were brought home to Jamaica, and he was inducted as a National Hero.

Veteran of the times in Kingston

In 1972, however, the left-wing PNP was elected with a massive majority. Michael Manley, son of Norman, led the party and pushed for policies that brought Jamaica closer to independent nonaligned countries. Manley was criticised for political links to Fidel Castro's Cuba, foreign investment dried up, wealthy Jamaicans left the island and the economy declined. The uncertain and volatile situation led to gang violence, and Jamaica seemed to be heading for civil war. In 1980 the JLP returned to power following a campaign that ended with hundreds dead. Foreign investment began to trickle back.

POLITICS TODAY

In 1989 the PNP regained power under Michael Manley, whose policies had changed radically. From 1993, when Manley retired due to poor health, the PNP was led by Percival Patterson, Jamaica's longest serving Prime Minister. He was succeeded in 2006 by Portia Simpson-Miller, the party's first female leader. Her term of office was short-lived, however: the PNP was narrowly defeated in the 2007 elections by the JLP, led by Bruce Golding. Simpson-Miller returned to power in 2011, and on taking up the office suggested that the country should leave the Commonwealth and become a republic. Her term included the celebration of the 50th anniversary of the country's independence.

HISTORICAL LANDMARKS

***c*.4000–1000 BC** The first Amerindians arrive from South America.
1494 Christopher Columbus lands on the north coast of Jamaica.
1510 First Spanish settlement founded at Sevilla la Nueva.
1517 First boat carrying African slaves arrives at the island.
1655 British forces take the island from the Spanish. The Spanish free slaves, who head to the interior of the island.
1670 The Treaty of Madrid cedes Jamaica to England.
1739 Peace treaty with freed slaves (Maroons).
1700s The number of African slaves increases dramatically, with around 250,000 working on Jamaican plantations.
1838 Emancipation of enslaved people.
1865 Morant Bay rebellion seeks better conditions for the liberated slaves.
1938 Difficult economic conditions lead to the formation of the first trade unions and political parties.
1962 Jamaica declares independence led by the JLP.
1972 Victory at the elections for the left wing Michael Manley and PNP.
1980 The JLP returns to power, led by Edward Seaga.
1989 Michael Manley returns to power with free market policies.
1997 Michael Manley dies. The PNP return for a third term.
2006 P.J. Patterson retires. The PNP elects Portia Simpson-Miller as its first female leader and Jamaica's first female Prime Minister.
2007 After 18 years of PNP government, the JLP wins the elections.
2010 74 killed in Kingston during a state of emergency to arrest a suspected gang leader.
2011 Simpson-Miller's PNP wins a snap general election.
2015 Possession of marijuana for personal use decriminalised.
2016 Portia Simspon-Miller (PNP) loses the general election by a two seat majority to Andrew Holness (JLP). Holness is the first PM to visit Israel.
2017 Simpson-Miller resigns as a member of the parliament. Jamaica grants the first medical marijuana licenses. Employment rate hits a historic high.
2018 Jamaica announces a ban on single use plastic bags, straws and Styrofoam products.

The Blue Mountains

WHERE TO GO

The island of Jamaica is spectacularly beautiful, from its mountainous interior, lush forests and plentiful streams and rivers to the sandy beaches that frame the coast. You can kick back and relax on the seashore while admiring the view, or be more active and explore the wildlife at the bottom of a coral reef or at the top of a mountain peak. Wherever you go in Jamaica your senses will be bombarded by the sight of glorious landscapes, the pulsating bass tones of the music, the fragrance of brightly coloured tropical fruit and flowers, and the taste of spicy jerk meats and fish or a cold beer on a hot day.

In this chapter, we journey clockwise around the island, starting at the tourist capital of Montego Bay on the northwest coast. Sangster International airport is within relatively easy reach of all the main resort areas on the north and west coasts. Cruise ships also dock at the ports of Montego Bay, Falmouth, Ocho Rios and Port Antonio.

The twisting roads of the rugged interior mean that cross-island journeys to Kingston and the south coast used to take longer than expected, but the North Coast Highway and Highway 2000 changed that. These roads have created a better connection between Kingston, Montego Bay, Ocho Rios and Port Antonio. The Linstead to Moneague segment of Highway 2000 was opened in 2014, and the final 67 km (42 mile) was completed in 2016.

Soon come

Switch to Jamaican time. The phrase 'soon come' means that things will happen eventually. Don't be in a hurry for anything.

Fresh fruit for sale on the beach

MONTEGO BAY

The northern coast of the island has been the major focus of tourist development on Jamaica since the 1970s. Much of the burgeoning development has occurred here, and in some places this has changed the character of the landscape. However, there's no denying that this area has just about everything needed for a perfect holiday, whether you want to do nothing but sit on a beach, dive and snorkel along the coral reefs, enjoy sports, or explore the history and culture of the island.

Montego Bay, or 'MoBay' as it's called by the locals, is probably the most complete resort area in Jamaica, with its beaches, sports and shopping, along with a large number of hotels that cater to all budgets. The town is only minutes from the Sangster International airport (built as a US Air Force base during World War II), so there is no lengthy transfer to your hotel. The town is surrounded by a host of different sights and sporting facilities. Its disadvantage is a lack of attractiveness: Montego Bay is a rather soulless hodgepodge of sprawling development with no real character. But if you are here simply to have fun, you might not even notice.

DOWNTOWN

The resort sits on the east side of the wide bay, with the cruise port on the west. **Downtown Montego Bay** is located between the two. It is a jumble of loud and boisterous streets, full of people, dogs and goats breathing the fumes of hundreds of buses and cars. Vendors in makeshift shacks sell beer or cigarettes, and oil-barrel barbecues cook jerk chicken and burgers. The town centre is **Sam Sharpe Square** **A**, previously called Charles Square and The Parade, but renamed after the hero of the 1831 slave rebellion who was hanged for his part in the uprising. In one corner of the square are the **Cage**, an old prison lockup built in 1806 to

'DADDY' SAMUEL SHARPE

'Daddy' Samuel Sharpe (1801–32) was a literate slave and a lay preacher who lived on the Belvedere Estate, south of Montego Bay. Sharpe encouraged his congregation to lay down their tools until their grievances had been addressed. The resulting slave protest started peacefully at Christmas 1831, but turned violent. It was brutally suppressed, and Sharpe was executed on The Parade, now memorialised as Sam Sharpe Square. It has been argued that the reaction of the British public to the fate of the slaves and the rebellion's leaders led to parliamentary enquiries and the eventual emancipation of Jamaican slaves. Sharpe was honoured as a National Hero in 1975.

Local art, Montego Bay

house drunken sailors or runaway slaves, and the **Ring**, the site of the once-regular slave auction. The Civic Centre was redeveloped from the ruins of the 1804 court house. Following an extensive refurbishment, it reopened in 2014 as **Montego Bay Cultural Centre** (Tue–Sun 10am–6pm), home to National Gallery West (https://nationalgallerywest.wordpress.com) and National Museum West. It also has space for performing arts and houses a bistro and a gift shop.

Nearby, **Harbour Street Craft Market** Ⓑ is a constant buzz of activity. This is the place to come to check out the range of local handicrafts and souvenirs available on the island. The windows and doors of over 100 wooden cabins are bedecked with printed sarongs, T-shirts and carved masks. Try your hand at haggling and you're bound to get a better price than you thought.

THE BEACHES

Head east to the **Gloucester Avenue** 'Hip Strip' for the beaches and resort life. This is the heart of the action, with some of the busiest bars, loudest music and wildest water sports on the island. As you reach Gloucester Avenue, you'll pass the remains of the **Fort Montego**, with its small sturdy walls and heavy cannon that guarded the bay for many years. **Fort Montego Craft Park** is just behind the fort.

Most beaches in MoBay are private, which means you pay a small charge to enter. They are kept neat and tidy, with water sports facilities and areas for changing and showering. The first one along the strip is **Walter Fletcher Beach** ❻, which is busy at weekends and is home to Aquasol Theme Park.

Further along the strip is **Doctor's Cave Beach** (daily 8.30am–5.30pm; www.doctorscavebathingclub.com), the original Montego Bay beach developed in the Edwardian era when sea bathing became a popular pastime throughout the British Empire. It became a centre for wealthy and upper-class visitors and was donated to the town in 1906 by the original owner. It is still as popular as ever and the sand is sublime, but the cave after which the beach was originally named was destroyed in 1932 during a hurricane.

Cornwall Beach (daily 8am–6pm), another private beach with perfect sand, is behind the St James shopping mall. There is a bar, watersports, and beach volleyball facilities.

The cruise port, or **Montego Bay Freeport**, sits on an outcrop on the west side of the bay. It is a popular stop on cruise itineraries. This area is also home to the **Montego Bay Yacht Club** (www.mobayyachtclub.com), which hosts a number of yachting regattas through the year. You

Playing on the floating trampoline at Doctor's Cave Beach

can hire boats here to take a morning or full day out at sea for sport fishing or just a relaxing jaunt.

Montego Bay Marine Park (Howard Cooke Blvd; http://www.mbmpt.org/), established in 1991, covers the whole of Montego Bay from the high tide mark to a depth of 100m and includes two fish sanctuaries where fishing is prohibited. It covers an area of 15.3 sq km (6 sq miles) of reef, sea-grass and mangrove swamps, stretching from Rum Bottle Bay in the west to Tropical Beach by the airport in the east. A number of companies offer underwater tours in glass-bottomed boats or submersible craft, or you can rent snorkel or scuba gear to get a closer look yourself. These can be booked from the offices at **Pier 1** (www.pieronejamaica.com), a small marina with a seafood restaurant and an entertainment centre that sits in the middle of the bay between the beaches and the cruise port.

Yachts moored at Montego Bay

SOUTH OF THE BAY

South of Montego Bay there are a number of attractions that make enjoyable excursions, if you want to tear yourself away from the beach or book an outing from your cruise ship.

The **Barnett Estate** ❶, with its 18th-century great house, has been owned by the Kerr-Jarrett family since 1755. Nicholas Jarrett arrived on the island in 1655, and the family was at the forefront of economic and political activities on Jamaica for many generations. They once owned almost all the land on which Montego Bay now stands. You can tour the still-operating plantation in a jitney and visit the 18th century **Bellefield Great House** (tours by appointment: Mon–Thu 10am–3pm; www.bellefieldgreathouse.com), which offers 'Taste of Jamaica' tours, focusing on Jamaican cuisine.

En route for Anchovy

Near the town of Anchovy, in the hills above Montego Bay, **Rocklands Bird Sanctuary** ❷ (daily 10am–sunset; not recommended for children under five) offers a fascinating close-up encounter with the birds of Jamaica. The sanctuary began almost by accident in the late 1950s when founder Lisa Salmon moved here. She loved the hummingbirds that inhabited the garden and began to feed them so that they became friendly. Sugar water for the hummingbirds and seed for finches and other birds are provided so that you can feed them.

High in the hills 27km (17 miles) south of Montego Bay is **Belvedere Estate** ❸ (Mon–Sat). It is a working plantation producing a mixed crop of spices and fruits, but it also opens a fascinating window on plantation life during colonial times. The current owners have created an agricultural museum to demonstrate the traditional methods of crop production as well as everyday life on the plantation.

Rose Hall interior

EAST ON THE COAST ROAD

East along the main coast road from the Montego Bay area, there is a string of luxurious resort hotels with facilities such as golf courses and equestrian centres. Two shopping malls at Ironshore and Half Moon Resort have boutiques, gift shops and fast-food outlets. A number of sightseeing attractions lie along this route, which leads to Falmouth and, eventually, to Ocho Rios.

GREAT HOUSES

Rose Hall Great House ❹ (daily 9am–6pm; charge; www.rosehall.com) is, perhaps, the most infamous house in Jamaica. Set high on a hill above the coast with commanding views, it was started in 1750 by George Ash and named after his wife Rose. The house was completed in 1777–80 by John Palmer, Rose's fourth husband. It was a calendar house, with 365 windows, 52 doors and 12 bedrooms. It later became the home of Annie Palmer when she married into the family; it is Annie who has given the house its fame and reputation. She was allegedly a white witch with potent voodoo powers who had murdered three husbands and an unidentified number of lovers before she herself died under mysterious circumstances. Locals, who believed that the house was haunted by her spirit, buried her nearby so that she could be reunited with her body and rest in peace. It is now believed that her behaviour could have been the result of lead poisoning, from eating her meals off lead plates.

The house fell into ruin after emancipation. In 1965 it was bought by the Rollins family, who renovated the main building. Rich mahogany wood cut from trees from the surrounding estate was used for new floors and ceilings. The interior has been redecorated with fabrics and furniture dating from the late 1700s to Victorian times. The ballroom has a woven wall-covering that is a reproduction of an original by Philippe de la Salle, which he created for Marie Antoinette.

Further east, **Greenwood Great House** ❺ (daily 9am–6pm; www.greenwoodgreathouse.com) was once the property of one of the wealthiest and most powerful colonial families in Jamaica. The first Barrett family member came to the

Greenwood Great House

island with the invading English forces. His descendants were major landowners from the middle of the 16th century and played an important role throughout the colonial history of Jamaica, holding positions of great influence in the judiciary and administrative bodies. Another member of the family was Elizabeth Barrett, who married poet Robert Browning. She was born in England and never came to the island: the responsibility for working the plantation lands fell to her male relatives.

This house, begun in 1780, was only one of the Barrett properties in the area and was built for entertaining rather than for use as a home. It now belongs to the Betton family and has retained many original features and authentic touches. Furniture and art collected over the generations fills the house, but perhaps most fascinating is the collection of original musical instruments and machines used for entertainment before the advent of electricity. The library is the largest of any plantation house in Jamaica, with over 300 volumes, some dating back to 1697.

Just before the town of Falmouth is **Falmouth Swamp Safari** ❻ (tel: 954-3065), home to the indigenous Jamaican crocodile and other tropical creatures. This wetland area covers about 1.6 hectares (4 acres) of mangrove swamp and has been turned into a breeding centre for crocodiles. You can take a guided walking tour of the swamp to see hatchlings, juveniles and adult crocodiles. Scenes from the James Bond film *Live and Let Die* were filmed here.

FALMOUTH

Once an important port for the shipment of sugar, molasses and rum, **Falmouth** has many Georgian buildings dating from the 18th century. The Jamaica National Heritage Trust has declared the whole town a National Monument. It is home to the Historic Falmouth cruise ship port in Jamaica (created in 2011), which can

receive the huge Oasis class ships. The cruise ship pier area has been developed as an 18th-century concept town with cobbled streets, shops, boutiques, restaurants, bars and shady parks.

Excursions from Falmouth include rafting (daily 8.30am–4.30pm; www.jamaicarafting.com) on the **Martha Brae River** ❼. The river is 48km (30 miles) long, and the 1.5-hour raft ride covers 5km (3 miles) of navigable river that meanders through the lush countryside, where you can take in the verdant river banks and the peace and quiet. Each 9m (30ft) raft is hand-built by the raft captains to carry two adults. The rafts are made of bamboo from the surrounding countryside and can be used for only four months before they have to be replaced.

Overlooking the Martha Brae is the **Good Hope Great House** ❽ (http://goodhopejamaica.com), a fine example of a Georgian plantation house, furnished with antiques and with a commanding view of the surrounding countryside. Tours are available around the house and estate, with its old water wheel, kiln and other sugar mill ruins. Part of the Good Hope Estate is now also a hotel and an adventure park.

Just to the east of Falmouth is a small bay that comes to life at night. Referred to by several names (including 'Glistening Waters' and 'Luminous Lagoon'), it is officially known as **Oyster Bay** ❾. Once darkness falls, the water in the bay is filled with luminescent micro-organisms that glow when agitated. You can take an evening cruise to watch this fascinating phenomenon and dip a hand in the water to make it happen yourself. The restaurant at the edge of the water is popular for a meal after the boat trip.

COCKPIT COUNTRY

In the highlands and hinterlands south of Falmouth is **Cockpit Country** ❿, an amazing and almost impenetrable landscape of limestone plateau (or 'karst') pitted with holes and fissures that have created fantastic formations. Deep depressions and high outcrops are blanketed by layers of green vegetation and topped by a lush canopy of trees, making travel difficult and at times dangerous. It is here that the Maroon people chose to live after

DUPPIES AND OBEAH

Many Jamaicans believe in the powers of magic and the underworld. Periods of bad luck or ill health are often seen as evidence of witchcraft and spells put on individuals. 'Duppies' are spirits of the dead who come back to earth. Good or evil, they can be manipulated by those still alive for mischief or revenge; 'obeah' is the local term for this type of sorcery. Look for coloured paint around the windows of homes, intended to prevent spirits from entering.

they had been freed by their Spanish captors in 1655.

The ruins at Columbus Park

Even today there are few roads – this really is one of the last true vestiges of wilderness in Jamaica. Because much of the area is inhospitable to human activity, it is rich in birdlife and rare plant species that have disappeared from other parts of the island. You can find hundreds of caves in the limestone fissures, and some intrepid visitors go 'spelunking', exploring their watery interiors. If you want to investigate the caves take an experienced guide and go well prepared.

Scattered Maroon villages remain, their inhabitants still making a meagre living out of the poor soil. Tours of the village of **Accompong** and the native Amerindian cave drawings nearby are organised by Cockpit Country Adventure Tours and the South Trelawny Environmental Agency (tel: 876-393-6584; www.stea.net). One of the best times to visit is in early January, when the Maroon people hold a major festival.

DISCOVERY BAY AND RUNAWAY BAY

Further east along the coast lies **Discovery Bay**, said to be the place where Columbus landed in 1494 on his second journey from Spain. The precise location is still disputed, as some say that he landed further along the coastline. Nevertheless, a small park on the roadside at Discovery Bay stands as a

Green Grotto Caves

tribute to his achievement. **Columbus Park** ⓫ is built on land donated by the Kaiser Bauxite Company, whose industrial site now dominates the bay. The Park includes an eclectic collection of objects from the history of Jamaica: old railway memorabilia, artefacts from sugar cane processing plants and a banana-tallying machine can all be found here.

The mammoth **Green Grotto Caves** ⓬ (daily 9am–4pm; www.greengrottocavesja.com), just outside Discovery Bay, are easily accessible and safe to explore. The system stretches up to 16km (10 miles) inland and includes Green Grotto, a vast cavern with an underground lake where stalactites are clearly reflected in the crystal clear water, and Runaway Cave. Amerindian paintings, though fading, can still be seen on the walls of the caves. Guided tours include a boat trip on the lake.

Runaway Bay ⓭ is the appropriately named area of coastline from where the last Spanish governor fled to Cuba as the British invaders closed in. Today Runaway Bay is one of the most popular resorts on the northern coast. A series of hotel complexes has sprung up to take advantage of the fine beaches. The diving and snorkelling opportunities along the reef wall here are said to be the best in Jamaica. Most hotels offer instruction and organised dives out to **Ricky's Reef** or the **Canyon**, two major reef areas. There are also a couple of small aircraft lying offshore (relics of drug runners who ran out of luck) that make a fascinating artificial dive site called **Ganja Planes**.

In the hills south of Runaway Bay is the tiny village of **Nine Mile**, where the singer Bob Marley was born and spent the early part of his life. Marley's body was brought here after his death and lies in the **Bob Marley Mausoleum** ⓮ (daily 9am–5pm), where he is buried with his prized guitar. The tombs of his mother and half-brother are also here.

The surrounding land and the tree under which he sat as a child have been turned into a shrine to the singer, but the ambience is spoiled by the numerous 'guides' and souvenir sellers who crowd your path to the entrance. Inside the compound you'll find genuine Rastafari guides, but here, too, it is very commercial, and not to everyone's taste. The whole site is painted in the bright green, red and yellow Rastafari colours that represent nature, blood and sunshine. The mausoleum lies in a small church with other symbols of Rastafari way of life, including a photograph of Haile Selassie (their spiritual leader) and the lion of Judah depicted in a stained glass window.

ST ANN'S BAY

To the east is **St Ann's Bay**, birthplace of the political leader and activist, Marcus Garvey. His statue can be found on Main Street, outside the town library. St Ann's Bay is also the site of **Sevilla la Nueva** ⓯, the original Spanish settlement on Jamaica, founded in 1509, which sits just to the west of the modern town. It is one of the oldest populated areas on the island, where Amerindian settlements have been found dating back to AD600. The Spanish settlers built a sugar factory here before 1526 and attempted to develop the site, but the persistent fevers contracted from mosquitoes in the swamps forced them to move and create a new capital at Spanish Town in 1538. However, Sevilla la Nueva was not completely abandoned, continuing as a working plantation and rum distillery that were later developed and expanded under British rule. The most obvious remains at the site date from this time. There are vestiges of the rum distillery, cattle pens and a large pimento barbecue for roasting allspice berries. Older remains lie scattered along the shoreline and in shallow water beyond the tidal reach. The museum in the English great house, **Seville Great House and Heritage Park** (daily 9am–4pm; www.jnht.com), displays finds from the site and hosts a historical exhibition.

OCHO RIOS TO ANNOTTO BAY

Jamaica's second tourist town **Ocho Rios** began in the 1960s when a fishing village was developed with the aim of turning it into a resort. There are several large hotel complexes here and the town is also a popular destination for cruise ships.

Though not the prettiest town on the island, Ochi', as it is known, has beautiful natural attractions nearby and makes a good base for excursions around Jamaica, being within easy reach of Kingston, the Blue Mountains (see page 60) and the coast road that leads to Montego Bay (see page 28) and Port Antonio

Eight rivers

Although Ocho Rios translates as 'eight rivers' in Spanish, the name is thought to be a mistranslation of the Spanish *'las chorreras'*, meaning 'river rapids'. There are plenty of waterfalls here but not eight rivers.

Glass-bottomed boats at Turtle Beach

(see page 52). There is little left of old Ocho Rios: the scant remains of **Ocho Rios Fort** are probably the oldest and now lie in an industrial area, almost forgotten as the tide of progress has increasingly swept over the town.

The main waterfront area, **Turtle Beach** Ⓐ, sits in front of the town centre. It is a wide arc of sand, shallow and sheltered. The beach is kept clean and there are facilities and refreshments available. You can hire a boat to take you snorkelling around the reef that runs all along the coast here, just a few hundred metres from the shore. Two massive all-inclusive resorts, the Moon Palace Jamaica Resort and the Riu Ocho Rios, overlook the beach.

Ocho Rios is a shopping mall for cruise-ship passengers. There are a number of expensive jewellery and other duty-free shops, all with goods priced in US dollars (duty-free goods must always be paid for in foreign currency). It's a veritable treasure-trove of

Climbing Dunn's River Falls

quality gems, gold and cigars. Take a look around the incongruous pink Taj Mahal shopping mall or Soni's Plaza in the centre of town. The latter complex, with over 100 shops, probably has the widest choice. There is also a thriving craft market behind the main beach, where you will be able to haggle for locally produced goods, from a T-shirt to a necklace of semi-precious stones. Once the business day stops, there are few bars and restaurants in the town; evening activity tends to focus on the large hotels.

Ocho Rios is surrounded by not only areas of natural beauty but also by landscaped tropical splendour. Nestled on the hillside above the town, **Shaw Park Botanical Gardens** ❸ (tours daily 8am–4pm; charge; tel 974-2723), admired among gardening connoisseurs, has wonderful views; it comprises 10 hectares (25 acres) of tropical plants and natural waterfalls that once formed the grounds of the Shaw Park Great House, which later became a hotel.

DUNN'S RIVER FALLS

This place of fantastic natural beauty and flowing water that epitomises the Amerindian name for Jamaica, *Xaymaca* ('land of wood and water') is unfortunately a victim of its own popularity. Only 5km (3 miles) west of Ocho Rios, **Dunn's River Falls** ⓰ (daily 8.30pm–4pm, from 7am on cruise ship days; www.dunnsriverfallsja.com) is a series of limestone cascades surrounded by overhanging vegetation that carry the water of Dunn's River almost to the sea.

Lines of people, all holding hands, do a slightly wobbly 'conga' to the top, where everyone forgets decorum and gets wet in the pools. You'll be lucky if you have the pools to yourself to enjoy the kind of romantic experience advertised in the tourist brochures as the Falls attract thousands of visitors each year and are packed with tour parties and cruise ship visitors.

Guides are optional, but they are sure-footed and will take care of your camera until you reach the top. Don't forget to take a change of clothing and a towel. There are wooden walkways at the side of the Falls for those who don't want to get drenched.

Splashing around in the Falls

RIVERS AND PLANTATIONS

The road leading south from Ocho Rios climbs out of the town and twists and turns through a narrow valley of tropical vegetation called **Fern Gully** ⓱. 5 km (3 miles) of giant cottonwood trees, with their tangle of thick roots, frame varieties of giant fern to create a canopy of fronds and leafy branches over the road. Insects, frogs and birds call together in a cacophony of sound. It feels so humid in the midst of the vegetation that you can imagine being on the set of a prehistoric dinosaur film. The canopy is so thick that very little light penetrates through.

Twenty minutes' drive from Ocho Rios, in the parish of St Mary, is **White River Valley** ⓲. This nature retreat offers tubing, horse riding, kayaking and hiking along forest trails and the chance to sample a sumptuous Jamaican meal (http://chukka.com). The **White River** runs east from Ocho Rios and marks the boundary between St Mary Parish and St Ann Parish. There are freshwater lagoons, rivers to swim in and picnic spots, as well as a restaurant and souvenir shop.

On the main coast road east out of Ocho Rios is **Prospect Plantation** ⓳ (www.prospect-villas.com), which offers tours by open-air jitney, horse trails and camel-trek trails through crops of coffee, bananas, allspice, plantains, sugar cane and many other crops. The guides at the plantation will give you plenty of information about the natural and introduced flora of the island. Visitors can also visit the butterfly house and feed ostriches.

The Spanish settled the land and grew crops here in the 17th century, but the fine Great House was built by English colonists in the 18th century. The plantation was bought in 1936 by English industrialist Sir Harold Mitchell and became an important focus for diplomatic, political and social activities in Jamaica.

Many important dignitaries have visited the house, including Sir Winston Churchill, and it has become a tradition for trees to be planted to mark each special occasion. The tour

Tubing along White River

passes trees planted by the Royal family of Luxembourg, US civil rights activist Andrew Young and the Duke of Edinburgh, among many others. You can plant your own tree as well. The plantation also houses a private academy for young people, the brainchild of Harold Mitchell. It promotes the ideal of good citizenship through hard work and community service. Many former academy students have gone on

FIREFLY AND ANNOTTO BAY

The coastal road continues east through the small town of **Oracabessa**, with its decaying iron fretwork, and on to **Galina Point**, the most northerly part of Jamaica. Set high on a bluff overlooking the coastline at Galina Point is **Firefly** ⑳ (daily; www.firefly-jamaica.com), the former home of Noel Coward, doyen of British theatre and cinema, and the archetypal Englishman.

Now managed as a museum by Island Outpost on behalf of the Jamaican National Trust, Coward had the house built in 1956 and lived here until his death in 1973. He is buried in the garden, at his favourite spot overlooking the sea. The house is surprisingly small and simple, with one bedroom, a tiny kitchen and a couple of social rooms. What makes it special is its position, with magnificent views of the coastline east toward Port Antonio and southeast to the peaks of the Blue Mountain range.

The parties Coward held here were legendary. Film stars such as Elizabeth Taylor, Sophia Loren and Charlie Chaplin were entertained with songs at the grand pianos that still sit in the main room. Coward valued his private life, however, and guests were never allowed to stay overnight at Firefly. They were given guest quarters at Blue Harbour on the shore, where Coward lived before building Firefly.

Nearby is the house of another famous person, an author whose fictitious protagonist has taken on an almost real persona. **Goldeneye** ㉑ (www.goldeneye.com) was home to Ian Fleming when he wrote all the James Bond novels. Fleming came to Jamaica in 1942 while serving in British Intelligence, decided to settle here, and bought the property in 1946. Although Bond was noted for his bravery and prowess, he was in fact named after a man of very different talents: Fleming took the name of his '007' hero from the author of the book *Birds of the West Indies*, which had been researched and written a few years earlier.

Goldeneye and its villas and beach cottages are part of the Island Outpost boutique hotel chain. Alongside is the **James Bond Beach Club** with changing rooms, restaurant and watersports equipment hire.

Inland from Firefly is **Brimmer Hall Plantation** ㉒ (tours Mon–Fri 9am–4pm), a working plantation of 809 hectares (2,000

A sea view near Oracabessa

acres) that produces a variety of crops, including bananas, coconuts and citrus fruit. It has a beautiful, single-storey great house, made (unusually) of wood and filled with an eclectic collection of furniture from the colonies of the British Empire. The tour, by jitney, shows how the plantation works, with knowledgeable staff to answer questions and give demonstrations of such skills as the correct technique for climbing coconut palms.

The main road continues to hug the north coast, but just before reaching Annotto Bay there is a turn south in the direction of Kingston. Take this route to reach **Castleton Botanical Gardens** ㉓ (daily 5.30am–6.30pm, Oct–Feb until 6pm; www.jnht.com) some 18km (11 miles) inland. The 37 hectares (91 acres) of gardens are set on lands above the Wag Wag River, which twists through a steep and narrow valley.

The gardens were landscaped in 1862 with a large consignment of plants from Kew Gardens in London. Beautiful exotic plants from every corner of the British Empire were subsequently brought here before being transplanted to other gardens on the island. It might not be the oldest, but Castleton is regarded by many as the 'father' of tropical gardens in Jamaica thanks to its work in the propagation and distribution of new plant genera.

JAMAICA'S BEST BEACHES

Long Bay (Negril). Commonly known as Seven Mile Beach, with fine, golden sand gently sloping into shallow water. Low-rise development leaves room for hundreds of palm trees.

Booby Cay (Negril). Lying just off Long Bay, this tiny island provides sand all around its rocky interior.

Doctor's Cave (Montego Bay). The original tourist beach is still as popular as ever, with lots of activities. Come and be sociable.

Lime Cay (Port Royal). Just think 'Robinson Crusoe' and you'll have the right idea. But avoid it at weekends, when it's more like Grand Central Station.

Turtle Beach (Ocho Rios). Everything is in one place, and you get a great view of cruise ships arriving and departing.

Frenchman's Cove (Port Antonio). Fine white sand in sheltered coves, with lots of tropical vegetation. Wander through the coral outcrops to find a private corner.

Long Bay (eastern tip). Just the place for long romantic walks, as rolling waves break on miles of pink sand. Not suitable for swimming because of the dangerous undertow.

Holland Bay (eastern tip). A stretch of fine white sand with not another soul in sight.

Treasure Beach (south coast). With numerous fishing boats, this dark volcanic sand beach is not just for tourists.

PORT ANTONIO AND THE EAST

Island hibiscus

The eastern area of Jamaica is the most tropical and most beautiful part of the island. The high peaks of the Blue Mountains dominate the landscape. This is where lush rainforest mixes with plantations of coffee on the high mountain slopes and meets thousands of banana plants that blanket the coastal plain. The mountains attract moisture sweeping across the Atlantic Ocean and are thus often cloaked in heavy rain clouds that feed the forests and fill numerous streams and rivers. There are few major roads in this area. The main route follows the coastline, circumventing the mountains and leading to some of the least-visited areas of Jamaica that are totally off the tourist track.

The western approach to Port Antonio is characterised by huge groves of banana plants, which in earlier times made the town one of the richest in the Caribbean. All along the northern coast here you will see remains of the old railway line, which once linked the plantations to the port but now mostly provides a place for children to play or animals to graze. The station houses, however, still give an impression of the grandeur of the recent past. The line was closed in 1985, but with the speed at which the native plants have reclaimed the land, it might have been 100 years ago.

Errol Flynn Marina at Port Antonio

PORT ANTONIO

Port Antonio dates from 1723, when the town was called 'Titchfield' after the English estate of the Duke of Portland, who was governor of Jamaica at the time. Expansion began after the 1739 peace treaty with the Maroons, who lived inland south of the site. The area proved unsuitable for sugar cane production, but in 1871 fruit shippers began to take locally grown bananas back to Boston in the United States, and the trade was an immediate success.

In its heyday, Port Antonio was the undisputed 'banana capital of the world', with an additional benefit: the banana boats brought the first tourists to Jamaica. The wealthy visitors travelled out on the empty boat and stayed in the area after the ships took their ripening cargo back to the US or England. Fine hotels catered to the visitors' every need, and the town revelled in the money brought in from abroad.

Those days are long gone, as is the booming banana market: exports from South and Central America broke the Caribbean monopoly in the 1970s. However, Port Antonio harbour still has a buzz of activity, especially in the harvesting season, as all of Jamaica's banana exports leave from here. The manual counting of the 'hands' and 'bunches' of bananas (recounted in Harry Belafonte's *Banana Boat Song*) was mechanised in the 1960s, but the work of loading the boats is still labour intensive. Developments at Port Antonio include the Errol Flynn Marina, designed to blend in with the town's architecture and the West Harbour's charm. It is the centre for sport fishing, and plays host to the International Blue Marlin Tournament every October, when the harbour is filled with sport-fishing boats from around the Caribbean.

Nestled against the Blue Mountains, the town has a beautiful setting. Two wide bays offer natural harbours, and tiny **Navy Island** sits just offshore. This was the island bought by Errol Flynn when he settled in Port Antonio in 1946; he used it as a garden extension for the large yacht he moored there. His drinking parties were legendary, and he is fondly remembered as a charming rogue. Navy Island is closed to the public.

A taste for sugar cane

Tropical fruit at the market

The headland between the two main bays is called '**The Hill**'; here you will find the oldest part of town. The houses of wealthy Port Antonio residents sat away from the bustle of the busy port in a grid of seven or eight streets. This area has fallen into decay, but there are still vestiges of its fine history to be seen. Ornate ironwork now rusts, wooden fretwork moulds and paint peels, yet there remains a beauty about this aging finery. Nearby on St George's Street is **St George's Village**, a shopping precinct designed as a quaint and quirky take on European architecture.

For a wonderful view of the whole town, take the road up to **Bonnie View Plantation Hotel** (closed). The twin harbours, Navy Island and the Hill, can be seen from here.

WEST OF PORT ANTONIO

The **Rio Grande** ㉔, just west of Port Antonio, is the largest river complex on Jamaica, combining a number of tributaries from the Blue Mountains. Rafts have long been a method of transport for local people, who use them to carry bananas down from the upper slopes to the port. Rafting on the Rio Grande was popularised by Errol Flynn and became a 'must' for tourists in the late 1940s – it is still popular today. The lush river valley cuts deep into the heart of the mountains, with sheltered habitats for birds and butterflies. A raft trip here is a more tropical experience than on the Martha Brae River (see page 37). Rafters start at Berridale and complete their cruise at Rafters' Rest (St Margaret's Bay). Stop for a snack or a hike along the way.

16 km (10 miles) west of Port Antonio are **Somerset Falls** ㉕ on the Daniel River in Hope Bay. Hidden in the rainforest, the falls plunge through a narrow gorge. Somerset is an old sugar plantation now with lovely gardens on the banks of the river. There are lots of facilities with a swimming pool, river pools and falls. A concrete path to the falls takes you past the ruins of a Spanish aqueduct and Genesis Falls, before reaching Hidden Falls. Here you can get on a boat to go behind the tumbling water into the cave or swim in the pools. The restaurant and bar get lively on Sundays with reggae, dominoes and dancing. Across the road, the

Rafting on the Rio Grande

river runs over Likkle Portie beach, where there is a lifeguard and a restaurant serving fresh fish meals.

EAST OF PORT ANTONIO

The drive east from Port Antonio offers some of the prettiest views in Jamaica. A series of coral headlands covered in tropical vegetation reach out into the ocean. Beautiful private villas and a small number of fine resort hotels sit proudly on the headlands or nestle in the small bays. **Frenchman's Cove** ㉖, a little further east, has a beautiful sandy and shady beach, accessed through the resort (entry charge that can include lunch on the beach; daily 9am–5pm; www.frenchmanscove.com). Tiny bays of soft sand sheltered by cliffs and cooling vegetation provide a completely different experience from the beaches of Montego Bay. This is

Frenchman's Cove

the area for romantic private getaways. **San San** gained a reputation in the days of Errol Flynn for its elegant social scene; today it is an exclusive hideaway with a fine golf course. A small faded sign points the way to **Blue Lagoon**, a tiny coastal inlet with a freshwater spring just offshore. The freshwater hole is said to be bottomless, although the diver-explorer Jacques Cousteau dived here and measured the depth at 61m (200ft). Beware of touts charging non-existent fees.

Boston is best for jerk meat

JAMAICA'S EASTERN TIP

If you continue along the main coastal road, you'll reach **Boston Bay**. This small fishing town is the traditional centre of 'jerk', Jamaica's national dish that has a worldwide following. The jerk marinating technique was first developed by the Maroon people as a method of tenderising and cooking their pork. You will smell the roasting meat and aromatic wood fires as you arrive in the village. The fresh pork is cut into 'bellies' and scored to make it easier to cook and serve. It is then covered in the paste that gives jerk its name, placed on a rack over the pit fire and turned every few minutes until it is ready. The marinade is a good deal spicier than you would find in a tourist restaurant, but the meat is wonderfully tender; ask for a bite-sized sample before you buy. Roasted breadfruit with the jerk provides the perfect bland antidote to the spice.

The Maroon community, descendants of proud and tenacious slaves, still live in two isolated pockets on Jamaica. **Moore Town** and **Cornwall Barracks**, hidden behind the John Crow Mountains and reached by a road from Port Antonio, make up the nucleus of the eastern group (the western Maroon area is in Cockpit Country, south of Falmouth). The settlements here were founded in 1739 after the peace treaty with the British. Maroon people are very private, still running their own affairs and paying no land taxes to the government. Although their villages don't look very different from the other rural communities on the island, it is the Maroon attitude to life which makes these societies interesting to visit. If you wish to get to know the people, you can arrange to visit them with a guide (see page 124).

The coastal road makes its way around the unspoiled eastern tip of Jamaica. The long journey from the major resorts means that few visitors venture this far.

Long Bay ㉗ is one of the longest and most magnificent beaches on the island, nature at its best. There is no development here for two main reasons. First, this sector of coastline is most at risk from the threat of hurricanes as they whip across the Atlantic Ocean and into the Caribbean Sea. Second, the coastal swells here are extremely dangerous, preventing swimming and water sports, although there is surfing for the intrepid. You'll find wooden fishing boats pulled up on the sands and nets hanging out to dry. The beach has

Maroon festival

On National Heroes Day (third Monday in October) Maroons descend upon Moore Town to honour Nanny, the founder of the town and legendary 18th-century chieftainess of the Windward Maroons.

fine pink sand and powerful breakers throw sea spray into the air. There are several beach bars that are good for lunch, and where you can sit and admire the dramatic view.

Reach Falls

Farther south, near the fishing village of Manchioneal, are **Reach Falls** ㉘ (also known as Reich Falls; Wed–Sun 8.30am–4.30pm, July–Aug daily 8.30am–6pm). There are toilets, changing facilities and concrete steps going down to the falls, but little else. The fresh clear water comes directly down from the mountains of the John Crow National Park and falls into a deep azure pool.

On the easternmost tip of Jamaica stands the isolated **Morant Point Lighthouse**, built in 1841. With pristine mangrove swamps and the deserted sandy beaches of **Holland Bay** and **Mammee Bay**, the landscape is truly magnificent. The land stretches out for miles.

From Morant Point, the road turns west back toward Kingston. There is little to hold the attention here although the area has seen important historical events. **Port Morant**, a little way west, was the place where Captain Bligh of *The Bounty* fame first landed breadfruit on Jamaica. The famous mutiny occurred during the first journey, when he refused the crew much-needed water, keeping it instead for the precious plants. Even after all his effort, however, only one plant survived and he had to return with a second cargo. It proved to be worth the effort for Bligh, who received a reward of 1,500 guineas.

Morant Bay is the major settlement in southeast Jamaica; it played a big part in one of the turning points in the history of the island. The Morant Bay rebellion of 1865 was led by Paul Bogle and supported by George William Gordon (after whom Gordon House, the Jamaican seat of Government, is named). The uprising and the violent reaction of the British forces resulted in the destruction of many of the historic buildings in the town, which never really recovered.

THE BLUE MOUNTAINS

Covering much of the interior of the eastern part of the island are the magnificent **Blue Mountains**, the highest on Jamaica. There are five major peaks ranging from John Crow Mountain at 1,753m (5,750ft) to Blue Mountain Peak at 2,256m (7,402ft). The mountains are blanketed with thick forests watered by regular tropical downpours from the heavy clouds that surround the high peaks. The blue heat haze that surrounds the mountains and gives them their name can best be seen on warm afternoons, when it is possible to see peak after peak stretching into the distance.

A number of slopes and valleys have remained untouched by man and offer a habitat for rare flora and fauna including the national bird, the streamertail hummingbird (commonly called

Bogle

The historic court house in Morant Bay is a reconstruction of the one burnt down during the 1865 rebellion. Paul Bogle and his brother were hanged from the centre arch of the gutted building. It has not been restored since a second fire in 2007. The courthouse is located in a modern building at 16 Church Street in St Thomas.

View over the Blue Mountains

the doctor bird), and the giant swallowtail butterfly (*Papilio homerus*), the largest in the Western Hemisphere. The richness of the environment around the Blue Mountains has long been recognised; the **Blue Mountains and John Crow National Park** ㉙ (www.blueandjohncrowmountains.org) was established in 1993 to manage and protect 78,212 hectares (193,292 acres) of land being damaged by illegal loggers and slash and burn farmers.

The best way to view the Blue Mountains is to drive from Buff Bay on the north coast down to Kingston on the B1 highway, although the road can be impassable after heavy rain due to landslides. Always check road conditions before you depart. The interior of the mountain range and the most beautiful parts of the parks are not accessible to vehicles: the best way to experience them is to take a guided walk. There are a variety of routes, which can last from a morning to several days. The hike to **Blue Mountain Peak** itself is not for the inexperienced and will take a full day; if you want to see the sunrise, start out at 2am to reach the summit in time to greet another Jamaican day (see page 124). Whichever option you choose, remember to take some warm clothing, because temperatures here are a few degrees lower than on the coast, even on a sunny day. When the clouds come in, it can feel quite chilly.

In addition to their tropical splendour, the Blue Mountains have slopes which are perfect for growing coffee. Blue Mountain coffee is said by aficionados to be the best in the world. The **coffee plantations** lie in the humid heights, at altitudes of 915–1,676m (3,000–5,000ft), where soil conditions and the slow growing process (five years from germination to harvesting) produce a fine crop with a high yield. This natural affinity between the Blue Mountains and the coffee bean is amazing, because the first plants are said to have arrived in Jamaica by accident.

In 1723 Louis XV of France sent three *Arabica* coffee plants to the French island of Martinique, which lies farther south. A few years later the Governor of Jamaica, Sir Nicholas Lawes, imported a coffee plant and some beans from Martinique and these were the start of the Jamaican coffee industry, the most important business in this part of the island for more than 250 years. Because of the topography and the delicate nature of the plants, much of the work is still done by hand and traditional working practices have endured. Note that coffee grown below 915m (3,000ft) is

Mountain coffee

Coffee beans normally take four months to develop from blossom to harvest, but in the Blue Mountains, where the weather is cool, damp and cloudy, they take 10 months, resulting in a harder, larger bean. The sugars in the bean caramelise on roasting, giving the unique flavour.

Kingston at night

called Jamaica High Mountain or Jamaica Supreme (or Low Mountain) and is not the same quality.

KINGSTON AND ENVIRONS

With one of the largest natural harbours in the world – lying between lush green hills and the Caribbean Sea – Kingston Bay became the perfect site for one of the biggest ports in the Caribbean. Commercial success made **Kingston** the capital of Jamaica in 1872.

Now home to about a quarter of the population of Jamaica, it is a huge city. Modern 'New Kingston', with its office buildings and high rise blocks, is the administrative heart of Jamaica, with government offices, consulates and boutiques. To the northeast lie the foothills of the Blue Mountain range, where wealthy Kingstonians build houses to take advantage of the cooling breezes. Those less well-off live on the flat, dusty plains below, where country life has simply been transplanted to the city. Goats wander the streets and people live in tin shacks with few amenities. They sit up against several other shacks that make up blocks of properties (or 'yards'). The violence and crime that have been a feature of life in Kingston over the years centre on political and gang rivalries within these yards.

DOWNTOWN

Downtown Kingston, once a model of British colonial 'pomp and circumstance', is now surrounded by some of the poorest and most densely populated neighbourhoods in the city. It is not a place to wander around at night. However, during the day the area is full of office workers going about their business and petty crime is no worse than in any other capital city. Take normal precautions.

JAMAICA'S 'HIGGLERS'

You'll meet these persuasive salespeople all over Jamaica, at craft markets or on the beaches. Their goal is to sell you the souvenir that you can't leave Jamaica without. However, since there are no set prices, you must engage in the intricate game of 'haggling' if you want to buy and not get ripped off.

Don't engage in haggling if you are really not interested in buying an article. It only creates bad feelings, and you may feel the sharp edge of a 'patois' tongue. A firm but honest 'No' is better than five minutes of negotiation followed by no sale. Higglers view this as disrespect for them on your part.

As a guideline, aim to start your negotiation at about half the initial price offered. Sale price should generally be about 20 percent lower than the vendor's original offer.

The city centre developed around the waterfront. Fruit, rum and spices were once transported from the old docks; today the harbour area has been transformed. In 1982, the **Jamaica Conference Centre** was built; there are also galleries and historical collections that celebrate the culture of the island. The **National Gallery** ⑳ (Tue–Thu 10am–4.30pm, Fri 10am–4pm, Sat 10am–3pm, last Sun of the month 11am–4pm; https://nationalgalleryofjamaica.wordpress.com/), at 12 Ocean Boulevard, has a comprehensive collection of Jamaican paintings, sculpture and other art, including works from the 1920s; there are many works by Edna Manley (1900–87), one of Jamaica's foremost modern artists, wife of Norman Manley and mother of Michael Manley, both former Prime Ministers. Beside the docks is the **Victoria Craft Market**, the domain of the famous 'higglers', the assertive women who run the small stalls. The building, constructed in 1872, is a fine example of Victorian colonial architecture.

Exhibit at the National Gallery

Away from the waterfront, the streets in the city centre feature a number of historic buildings. On Duke Street you will find **Headquarters House**, built in 1755. The house was selected as the seat of the island legislature in 1872, when the capital was moved from Spanish Town to Kingston. It is now the base of Jamaica National Heritage Trust. Nearby **Gordon**

House, built in 1960, is home to today's legislators; it was named after George William Gordon, leader of the Morant Bay Rebellion, who became a member of the Jamaica Assembly and spoke out for the rights of the poor and oppressed.

National Heroes Park, at the north end of Duke Street, used to be a racetrack (you can still make out the shape of the circuit). All of Jamaica's national heroes are buried here with impressive monuments symbolising their lives and achievements: Sir Norman Manley and his artist wife, Edna, Sir Alexander Bustamante, George William Gordon, Sam Sharpe, Marcus Garvey and Nanny of the Maroons, while the north section is reserved for the burial of former prime ministers and other individuals who have contributed to the political and educational development of the country.

The **Institute of Jamaica** (http://instituteofjamaica.org.jm), 10–16 East Street, was founded in 1879 to encourage research in science, art and literature in the true spirit of the Victorian age. It's home to the **National Museum of Jamaica**, which reopened in 2013 after renovation and expansion with the country's first ever exhibition on the Rastafari movement (Mon–Thurs 9am–4pm, Fri until 3pm; http://museums-ioj.org.jm). The complex also houses the **Natural History Museum** (Mon–Thu 9am–4.30pm, Fri until 3pm; http://nhmj-ioj.org.jm), entrance on Tower Street, the oldest museum on the island. The herbarium has a collection of over 130,000 specimens of flowering plants, algae, fungi, lichens, mosses and ferns. The **National Library** (Mon–Thu 9am–4.30pm, Fri 9am–3.30pm; www.nlj.gov.jm) next door to the Institute has the largest collection of books, articles and papers on the history of the West Indies and is an important archive.

King Street is the heart of the city centre and the main shopping street. Here is **William Grant Park**, originally Victoria Park, in reality a small town square that was opened in 1879 with a life-sized statue of Queen Victoria at its centre. In 1977, it was renamed after the nationalist leader. The **Parade**, the streets surrounding the park, once heard the marching steps of British soldiers; it was here that slaves were beaten or hanged as punishment for their 'crimes'. Now it is a hive of 'higgler' activity and the hub for bus routes around the city.

Devon House

NEW KINGSTON

New Kingston is the modern commercial centre of the Corporate Area (parishes of Kingston and St Andrew), and is the hub of business, with hotels, fast food places and night spots. Near the Jamaica Pegasus hotel is **Emancipation Park**, popular with the lunch crowd in the day and joggers in the evening.

On the edge of the district is **Devon House** (mansion tours Mon–Fri 9.30am–5pm, gardens daily 9.30am–10pm, shops Mon–Fri 10am–6pm, restaurants until 10pm; https://www.devonhouseja.com), built in 1881 as a plantation house for George Steibel, the first Jamaican millionaire. The beautiful exterior is complemented by the fine period furniture housed inside. The mansion was renovated in 1967, 1982 and again in 2008. The gardens are a cool place to sit, and the stables and outbuildings have been converted into a

Bob Marley Museum

lovely courtyard containing attractive shops, cafés, an ice cream parlour and a notable restaurant. Some shops and eating places are open on Sunday.

Nearby on Hope Road are **Jamaica House**, containing the offices of the Prime Minister; **Vale Royal**, the Prime Minister's official residence; and **King's House**, home of the Governor General, originally the residence of the Bishop of Jamaica. None of these grand buildings is open to the public.

Tuff Gong Recording Studios used to be located at 56 Hope Road, a small compound where reggae musician, Bob Marley, lived and worked. Since his death it has been transformed into the **Bob Marley Museum** (guided tours Mon–Sat 9.30am–4pm; www.bobmarleymuseum.com) and managed by the Marley family to protect the memory of his life.

The museum has some interesting displays, including Marley's gold records and photographs of activity at the studios. Some of his personal effects can be found in the modest bedroom where he slept.

PORT ROYAL

A spit of land reaches out south of the city across Kingston Bay, sheltering the famous harbour. Called the **Palisadoes** (after the Spanish word *palizada*, meaning 'stockade'), this is an arid area of magnificent cacti and margins of mangrove that shelter populations of seabirds. Halfway along the narrow peninsula you'll find **Norman Manley International Airport**, the main airport of entry for Kingston and the eastern part of the island. At the tip of the Palisadoes is Port Royal.

When the British arrived in the late 1650s they built Fort Cromwell here; it was renamed **Fort Charles** following the restoration of the British monarchy in 1662. **Port Royal**, the town surrounding the fort, earned a reputation as the most raucous and debauched city in the Caribbean. With the help of the pirates who made the town their base, Port Royal became

JAMAICA'S PREDATORY PEST

If you travel around the island, you are bound to catch sight of a mongoose running across the road into the undergrowth. This small furry creature was introduced to Jamaica during colonial times to prey on snakes and rats, which were a danger both to the people and to the crops. The mongoose was extremely successful in ridding the island of these two problems. However, it then began to look for other things to eat. It is now considered to be the most populous and vicious pest on the island, preying on domestic chickens as well as eating the eggs and chicks of native wild birds.

a rich city, with the income from sugar and rum combined with stolen Spanish treasure (see page 16). After the 1692 earthquake that devastated the city and buried much of its wealth, Port Royal never fully recovered. Some treasures have been salvaged (along with everyday articles such as pewter cutlery and plates); much still lies only a few feet below the waves.

Kingston replaced Port Royal as the commercial centre of the island. However, Fort Charles was rebuilt as a military and naval garrison, and it protected Jamaica and much of the English Caribbean for 250 years until yet another earthquake struck in 1907. The brick fort, home to Lord Horatio Nelson during 1779, still stands proud and 'ship-shape'. The large cannons on the battlements now guard **Fort Charles Maritime Museum** ㉛ (daily 9am–5pm), which documents the maritime history of Jamaica. Here you can view models both of the fort and of the types of ships that sailed the Caribbean over the centuries.

Landslides and small quakes have taken their toll on sites at the Fort, and **Giddy House** is a perfect example of this. The small, square building once stored ordnance, but it has been left at a very precarious angle, sinking back into the sand. The **Old Naval Hospital** can be found a little farther to the north; its distinctive iron supports were brought to Jamaica in 1819 and were designed to be both earthquake and hurricane proof. The hospital building now houses the **National Archaeological and Historical Museum** ㉜, which displays a fascinating collection of finds from the sunken city of Port Royal.

Residents of the little village of Port Royal make their living from fishing. On weekends, it is popular with families from Kingston who come to enjoy the fresh air or a fried fish dinner at one of the little restaurants that spill out on to the streets. From the marina you can take a boat to **Lime Cay**, which lies just to the south of Port Royal. This tiny 'desert island' offers the chance to sunbathe on sandy shores or snorkel in clear water and feel a million miles away from Kingston.

CENTRAL HIGHLANDS AND THE SOUTH

Away from the large towns and tourist resorts, life continues in time-honoured tradition. In central and south Jamaica, numerous small settlements and family farms dot the countryside, where you'll see donkeys tethered at the roadside or trotting along the lanes carrying large baskets. A network of smaller roads that knit the villages together make travelling a real adventure: there are few signposts (and even fewer people) to point the way if you do become lost.

The south coast is peaceful and relatively undeveloped

The contrast between the landscape of the central highlands and the south coast could not be more marked. The highlands are cool, with green hills rolling through the heart of Jamaica. As you travel south the landscape changes. Acres of grassland surround coral limestone columns and escarpments. Low-growing acacia trees replace tropical vegetation, with the landscape characterised much more by prairie than by palm trees. The southern-most margins of the island – away from the pressure of human development – are a haven for wildlife.

SPANISH TOWN

The Spanish settlers in 16th-century Jamaica, having tired of the disease-ridden Sevilla la Nueva in the north, looked for a new site for their capital city. They chose the flatlands around the Rio Cobre and, in 1534, established Villa de la Vega, later called St Jago de la Vega. The British captured Jamaica in 1655 and henceforth gave the settlement the rather unimaginative name 'Spanish Town'. As capital of a wealthy colony, **Spanish Town** (http://www.jnht.com/site_spanish_town.php) had its fair share of fine buildings that included courthouses, administrative offices and official residences. However, the capital was moved in 1872 to Kingston, the commercial heart of Jamaica, and a malaise enveloped Spanish Town from which it never recovered.

The elegant Georgian buildings along the **Parade**, have fallen into disrepair. The most striking building in the Parade is the white stone edifice that houses the **Rodney Memorial** ㉝, constructed at great expense in gratitude after Admiral Rodney's fleet saved Jamaica by defeating the French at the Battle of Les Saintes in 1782. One wing houses the **Jamaica Archives and Records Office**, which preserves original documents from throughout the island's history.

On the west side of the square is **Old King's House** (built in 1762), which was the official residence of the British governor; it was here that the proclamation of emancipation was issued in 1838. It was a fine building was destroyed by fire in 1925. Only the façade is original; the building behind it is modern.

The **Jamaican People's Museum of Craft and Technology** (Mon–Thu 9.30am–4.30pm, Fri until 3pm), a branch of the National Museum of Jamaica, housed in a reconstructed corner of the house, features a model of how the building looked before the fire. The other two sides of this fine Georgian square are taken up by the ruins of the old Court House and what was the House of Assembly, now local government offices.

The **Hellshire Hills**, south of Spanish Town, come as a surprise to those who think that the tropics can only be lush and green. The landscape here is underscored by limestone and receives fewer than 760mm (30in) of rain per year.

There is little soil to support plants, resulting in a desert-like landscape of cactus and low scrub trees. The area has become the last haven for many of the native but almost extinct plants, animals, and birds of Jamaica. Here you'll find the last few Jamaican iguanas and yellow snakes.

Hellshire Beach

Cool Manchester

Manchester's cool climate (20°C/70°F in the summer and 16°C/60°F in the winter) appeals to Jamaicans returning to the island after decades living abroad in the UK and North America.

The string of white sand beaches along the coast is a popular destination with Kingstonians on weekends.

MANDEVILLE

Mandeville sits to the west of Spanish Town in the Don Figuero Mountains. Its cool air and pretty setting made it a favourite retreat for colonial families, right up to the end of British rule in Jamaica in 1962. They came to spend their weekends here, away from the hot and humid atmosphere of Kingston. Today, it is a favourite place for wealthy Jamaican families for very much the same reason. The town was laid out in 1816 and named after Lord Mandeville, the eldest son of the Duke of Manchester, after whom Manchester Parish was named. The English modelled the town and its buildings on those of their homeland, and one can imagine the village greens, tennis and golf clubs, and grassy verges taken from a typical London suburb.

There are a number of interesting attractions lying to the west of Mandeville. **Appleton Distillery** ❸❹ (tours Mon–Sat 9am–4pm) is situated in rolling hills just to the south of Cockpit Country. Sugar cane was brought to Jamaica by the Spanish in the early 16th century. Much of the crop was exported, but it was treated before being shipped and a by-product of the treatment was molasses, used as a basis for making rum.

Many major sugar factories had a distillery on site, usually producing alcohol for local consumption. Appleton Distillery, in operation since 1749, produces 42,000 litres (74,000 pints) of rum every day. Much of this is 'overproof' rum, the basis of intoxicating rum punches, but the finest rum is aged in casks for up to 30 years to produce a spirit comparable to brandy or cognac.

The distillery offers a tour of the rum plant to learn about its historical production and gives the visitor an opportunity to taste and buy.

In some parts of the island, bamboo was planted along the roadside to provide shelter for people travelling in the heat of the day. The groves of bamboo also created places where slaves would congregate without being seen by their masters. Much of the bamboo has since decayed or been dug up, but **Bamboo Avenue** ㉟, the one remaining section, can be found on the main A2 road between Mandeville and Black River. It is a 4km (2.5-mile) tunnel of bamboo surrounded by sugar cane, with somnolent grazing cattle tethered along its length.

Cascades at YS Falls

Nearby are **YS Falls** 36 (Tue–Sun 9.30am–3.30pm; www.ysfalls.com), found on a working thoroughbred horse stud and cattle ranch that dates from 1684. The water cascades 50m (164ft) over seven tiered falls and has formed two large pools and a small cave system at the base of the second drop.

The falls are surrounded by mature native forests and vibrant tropical flowers, but an area of grassy lawn has been created for sunbathing and picnicking. From the ticket office you get a jinty tractor ride to the falls complex, where there are changing rooms, toilet facilities, children's playground, bar, grill and gift shop. You can swim in some of the natural pools, and lifeguards on site will tell you which ones are safe. For more of an adrenaline rush, there is a canopy zip line from the top of the falls to the bottom and river tubing rides, both at extra cost.

It is said that the falls got their name from the initials of the two original landowners, John Yates and Colonel Richard Scott. The cattle and sugar barrels exported from the plantation had these initials branded onto them.

BLACK RIVER

Once a major port on the south coast, **Black River** is now a small, sleepy town on the banks of the river from which it took its name. Its industry was the export of red logwood and the dyes of indigo and Prussian blue, which were extremely valuable in Britain. There is still some fine Georgian architecture here, but most visitors come to see the **Great Morass Mangrove Swamp** 37, also called **Lower Morass**. This area, which should not be confused with the Great Morass near Negril, is about 32,375 hectares (80,000 acres) of freshwater and tidal wetlands. The Mangrove Swamp and rush beds are an important habitat for many species of birds and fish, as well as home to a small population of Jamaican crocodiles. Smaller than the Florida species and said to be more docile, they grow to 6m (20ft) in length and can live to an age of 100 years.

The Black River, at 71km (44 miles), is the longest in Jamaica; it was an arterial route used to transport rum and lumber from the inland plantations. It still provides a living for many families, either from fishing or from the harvesting of bullrushes for basket making. Tours on the river and into the Great Morass start from Black River town. The route takes you into the **Mangrove Alley**, said to be the quietest place in Jamaica, where you can search out the basking reptiles and native birds that call this place home. Roots, which look like cathedral organ pipes, drop from the higher trees. Your guide will turn off the engine and an eerie silence will envelop the boat. Choose a tour company according to your interests; some guides concentrate on seeing crocodiles while others give a more rounded wildlife tour.

Taking a break at Black River

TREASURE BEACH

The southern coastline of Jamaica has so far resisted the pressure from big developers, partly because it has few main roads. Those who do venture here are rewarded with beautiful scenery and friendly people.

Treasure Beach ㊳ is the only resort area to speak of, with just a handful of hotels stretching across three sandy bays and private coves, well-suited for snorkelling and swimming. There are also cottages for rent, which make this an idyllic spot for walkers and visitors who prefer a quiet getaway to the busy all-inclusive resorts on the north coast.

The local population of St Elizabeth Parish still makes a living from fishing and their wooden boats rest high on the dark, volcanic sand. You'll be able to spend the day relaxing without being hassled. If you want to buy a souvenir, just hail the mobile shop that drives slowly along the road looking for customers. There's very little to do here but chill out.

East of Treasure Beach are some beautiful strips of coast. On one is the Little Ochi seafood restaurant, a simple affair on the beach in the fishing village of **Alligator Pond**. The government-owned **Alligator Hole** (also known as Canoe Valley Wetland) on the eastern side of Long Bay has been awarded official status for protection of the last three remaining manatee on Jamaica. Watch out for them being fed by the local conservationists. This pristine region of freshwater and saltwater swamps, edged with limestone cliffs, offers a refuge to this gentle creature as well as to birds and land crabs.

The pool at Jake's, Treasure Beach

NEGRIL AND THE WEST

This area, the furthest from Kingston, lagged behind other parts of Jamaica in modern development, protected from the commercial activity of the east by the limestone landscape of Cockpit Country, making travel and communication difficult. It was an outpost of pirate activity in the 17th and 18th centuries. Today, Negril is at the forefront of the tourist industry.

Heading west from Montego Bay, the main road hugs the coastline. Just a little way out of town is **Tryall Estate** (www.tryallclub.com). The Georgian Great House has been used as a guest house since the 1930s to supplement falling income. The old plantation has now been transformed into the first (and some say the best) villa resort on the island. The manicured greens of the golf course can be seen on both sides of the main coast road, along with the plantation's water wheel.

NEGRIL

A pirate hideaway in the 1600s, **Negril** was rediscovered in the 1960s by the 'children of love' and others looking for an alternative lifestyle. It is now popular with 'spring breakers', US students seeking a party and a good time. Jamaicans say that Negril isn't a place – it's 'a state of mind' where almost anything goes. There are few hippies left today, but the pleasures are still pretty earthy: it's not unusual to see topless sunbathers or catch a faint whiff of 'aromatic' smoke. You're also more likely to see true Rastafari here, along with others who simply enjoy living the image of the religion without abiding by its strict rules. Dreadlocks and tams (colourful knitted hats) are everywhere, along with the passing salutations. Located on the western tip of Jamaica, Negril is also one of the best places in the world for watching the sun go down.

To the east, running north, is Long Bay, and **Seven Mile Beach** 39, a vast expanse of fantastic sandy beach, while to the west, heading south, is West End, with coral cliffs that drop directly into the clear blue ocean.

Long Bay is 11km (7 miles) of sublime fine sand, gentle azure water and cooling palm trees. It is one of the best beaches in the Caribbean, parts of which are public. Several large resort hotels have been built here but there are also small and intimate, family-run hotels if you want a more personal touch.

Vendors and hair braiders can be found in pink booths along the beach, but any number of 'unofficial' ladies who braid can be found at the cafés and bars.

Across Norman Manley Boulevard from the beach is **Kool Runnings Water Park** 40 (Tue–Sun 10am–5pm; http://koolrunnings.com/), an adventure park with action-packed attractions for all the family, including water slides of all shapes and sizes. At the northern end is the **Anancy Village** for dry land activities such as go-karting, a bungee trampoline, carousel rides, restaurants and bars.

At the top of Long Bay is **Booby Cay**, a small island just a short distance offshore. The tree-topped rock surrounded by

ALOE VERA

As you lie on the beach, you are sure to be offered an aloe vera massage by a passing 'higgler'. You will be told that it will help you develop a golden tan, but be aware that aloe – although an excellent treatment for sunburn – offers no sun-protection whatsoever and your skin will likely burn. Make sure that you use a product with a suitably high SPF while you sunbathe.

Catamarans on the beach at Negril

golden sandy beaches is the archetypal 'desert island' – a great place for snorkelling, sunbathing, or picnics. You can rent a canoe to get there under your own steam or take a leisurely ride in one of the many small ferry boats departing from Long Bay.

The coral cliffs of **West End** provide a total contrast to Long Bay. Diving and snorkelling are the things to do here among the rocks and caves, and the shimmering waters house some wonderful sea life. West End is also the place to take in the sunset. Tourists flock to **Barney's Hummingbird Garden** (daily 8.30am–5.30pm, www.barneyshummingbirdgardenjamaica.com), a little piece of blooming paradise full of these colourful birds, and almost everyone heads to **Rick's Café** ❹❶, (see page 113) perched on the cliff top, to have a drink and set up the camera. While you're waiting, you'll be entertained by the divers who launch themselves from the tops of tiny perches into the azure sea some 9m (30ft) below. They are often joined by courageous tourists, who usually get more applause than the professionals.

Alternatively, a sunset cruise on a catamaran will transport you effortlessly to West End, and you can lie offshore away from the crowds with your rum punch. The cliff road ends at the Victorian-era **Negril Lighthouse** ㊷, which still protects ships passing this rocky promontory.

To the east of Negril is the **Great Morass**, a wetland area covering around 2,400 hectares (5,900 acres). The wetland and the **Royal Palm Reserve** ㊸ preserves one of the largest swathes of Royal Palm – Jamaica's national plant – left on the island. Numbers have dwindled due to the rapid tourist development, but the palms here are now protected. The wetlands support a large number of birds and land crabs. There have

Cliff jumping at Rick's Cafe

been attempts to drain the wetlands, but this damaged not only the Great Morass but also areas of the coral reef offshore. Both are now officially protected.

TO THE SOUTH

The road along the coastline to the south travels through busy agricultural towns and fishing villages mostly untouched by tourism. The first settlement is **Little London**, which has a relatively large Indian population that provides the markets with much of Jamaica's fresh produce. Next is **Savanna-la-Mar**, the capital of Westmoreland Parish, where **Mannings School** (built in 1738) retains its original, brightly coloured, colonial-style wooden buildings, beautifully preserved – a perfect environment for the children in their smart uniforms. Nearby at Ferris Cross is **Paradise Park**, a working cattle ranch where you can go horse riding through the grounds and on the beach, planning to opening its first Paradise Park Solar Farm in 2019.

South of Savanna-la-Mar the road hugs the coast, here narrow beaches brim with faded wooden pirogue canoes and other boats. This was traditionally one of Jamaica's prime fishing areas, and around **Bluefields** you'd see local men carrying their catch home. A marine sanctuary in Bluefields Bay was established in 2009 in order to conserve stocks and prevent overfishing, which had posed a serious threat up until then.

Beyond here, at Brighton, is the **Blue Hole Mineral Spring** ㊹ (Mon–Thu 9am–11pm, Fri–Sun 9am–midnight, off-season shorter hours; www.blueholejamaica.com), where there is a 10.5m (35ft) deep blue hole you can swim in and a spring-fed swimming pool.

Nearby, at **Belmont**, is the **Peter Tosh Mausoleum** ㊺. Tosh, a reggae musician and guitarist in The Wailers, was a committed Rastafari before his murder in 1987.

Hiking in the rainforest

WHAT TO DO

Jamaica cannot claim to have the very best beaches, reefs, or sport fishing in the Caribbean. However, it is indeed one of the best 'all-around' islands in the region, offering a wide range of opportunities for a variety of activities. Under the warm island sun you can enjoy water sports or you can just relax on the sand doing nothing at all. Nightlife includes an abundance of reggae music and dancing, and if you're here at the right time of year you can attend some of the world's biggest music festivals. For those in shopping mode, the choices are many: woodcarvings, colourful clothing, coffee, and (of course) rum.

SPORTS AND OUTDOOR ACTIVITIES

BEACHES AND WATER SPORTS

Spending the day on the beach taking in the sun is one of the primary reasons tourists visit Jamaica. Every resort area has its own famous beaches with their own particular beauty. Many of the beaches are private, meaning that you must pay admission, but they are well maintained and offer lots of facilities. Negril has the great expanse of Seven Mile Beach on Long Bay and the small 'desert island' of Booby Cay, while Montego Bay has the shorter expanses of Doctor's Cave Beach and Cornwall Beach. In Ocho Rios you will find Turtle Beach, where you can watch the cruise boats docking at the pontoon in the bay. Port Antonio beaches are now the domains of the fine hotels on San San Bay, Frenchman's Cove and Dragon Bay, all of which are tiny coves protected by rocky tropical outcrops. Long Bay on the eastern coast is wonderful because it is remote and uncrowded, but it is not suitable for

Snorkelling in Negril

swimming because of the strong currents. Treasure Beach on the south coast has dark volcanic sand beaches that are home to colourful fishing boats.

At the major resorts, beaches are kept clean and facilities for a range of water sports are readily available. Jet skiing is popular in sheltered waters near the beaches. If you are adventurous, you can go parasailing, with a boat pulling you along above the beach and waterfront. This is particularly exciting along Long Bay at Negril. A couple of bars have even installed large trampolines offshore, where you can swim out and bounce above the water.

If you do intend to take part in any sporting activity, make sure to check that your travel insurance policy specifically covers it. Some policies have clauses that exclude certain sports.

Snorkelling

Jamaica is particularly good for snorkelling, with many reefs and rocky promontories to explore very close to the shore. There are also a number of shallow areas between reefs that offer a fascinating view of various types of sea life. Beautiful tropical fish in iridescent blues and greens search through the coral for food, and in deeper waters you can spot bigger fish such as rays and nurse sharks. All the major resorts have small boats offering trips to offshore sites if you want to snorkel in deeper water.

The West End at Negril is ideal for snorkelling. The coral cliffs drop down into a clear azure sea, and there are hundreds of caves and canyons to explore. Montego Bay has the Marine Park with a range of environments. At Doctor's Cave Beach you can snorkel in an area where warm spring water meets the sea, or join a guide to go further out to the Coyoba, Seaworld or Royal reefs where the fish are larger and more varied. Further east, Runaway Bay has fine reefs running parallel to the line of hotels along the beach. Ocho Rios has a wonderful shallow reef running east from Turtle Beach for safe snorkelling.

JAMAICA'S TOP DIVE SITES

Negril. Pete Wreck is an old submerged tug boat. Throne Room is a huge cavern with yellow sponges. Sharks' Reef is home to nurse sharks, while you can see eels at Rock Cliff Reef.

Montego Bay. The Marine Park contains underwater walls of coral. Airport Reef and Widowmaker's Cave are two of the most famous sites.

Runaway Bay. Ricky's Reef at a depth of 30m (90ft) is covered in gorgonians and lettuce coral, while Pocket's Reef is a wall dive covered in gorgonians, black coral and sponges. Ganja Planes has the wreckage of aircraft, which have now been colonised by sea creatures.

Ocho Rios. The reef wall drops over 900m (nearly 3,000ft) but comes close to shore, offering nearby dives with a variety of fish and other aquatic life. A deliberately-sunk former minesweeper, *Kathryn*, is now home to a range of marine life.

Kingston. To dive the sunken city of Port Royal you must obtain special permission. For information contact a local dive operator.

Diving

Much of the northern coast of Jamaica is fringed by areas of deep reef wall that make diving a pleasure. Although some sections of reef have been damaged in the last years, there are still many areas with a wide range of fish and other marine creatures to see. Most of the major resort areas offer diving opportunities and certified training facilities for those who want to learn how to dive. Your hotel may offer certified instruction or guided dives. For more information contact the Jamaica Tourist Board (see page 129) for a selection of approved and certified dive operators.

Boat Charters, River Tours and Rafting

If you don't want to get into the water but you'd still like to see aquatic life on the reef, then take a glass-bottomed boat trip. There are a number of companies in all the major resorts. At Negril and Ocho Rios, the boats tie up along the main beach; you can negotiate a price while you sunbathe. The boats in Montego Bay all dock at the same place, so you can compare prices and facilities. Pier 1 has a range of options, from small boats to large semi-submersible craft that will take you under the water in complete comfort. If you

Take a trip on a glass-bottom boat from Buccaneer Bay

are not a confident swimmer, a boat is probably the best way to enter this very different aquatic world.

Visitors can explore Jamaica's inland waters by raft on the Martha Brae River (see page 37) or Rio Grande (see page 54). Take a trip down the Black River to experience the Great Morass (see page 76; for tours contact Irie Safari, tel: 715-4167; www.iriesafariswampbuggys.com) and see crocodiles in action, or you can simply get wet and picnic at YS Falls (see page 76; tel: 997-6360; http://ysfalls.com), near Mandeville.

Sport Fishing

Sport fishing is also a popular activity. Port Antonio hosts a major international angling tournament each October. Blue-and-white marlin are the prized catch: the waters around Jamaica are especially rich in these magnificent fish and this is the oldest marlin-fishing tournament in the Caribbean. Other fish are plentiful, but the bounty of Jamaican waters is being threatened by overfishing. Respect efforts that are under way to create marine sanctuaries around the island. You will find sport-fishing boats for hire at the marinas in the major resorts: Bay Pointe at Montego Bay, the main beach in Ocho Rios, Morgan's Harbour Hotel at Port Royal in Kingston and Errol Flynn Marina at Port Antonio. You can hire a boat with equipment and crew by the day or half day.

OTHER ACTIVITIES

Golf

Jamaica has an excellent range of golf courses, from small nine-hole to championship 18-hole courses. Several important tournaments take place on the island during the year,

Golf at Sandals, Ocho Rios

where you can watch international players from the PGA and the LPGA compete.

Montego Bay has fine courses, professionally designed and maintained in peak condition. The most famous course is at the Tryall Club (www.tryallclub.com), west of Montego Bay, where the greens caress the undulating coastal slopes. To the east of Montego Bay, where the coastal plain is flat and wide and an ideal landscape for golf, there are several large hotels that have courses. The four best are the Half Moon Golf Club (www.halfmoon.com/golf), the White Witch course at Ritz Carlton Rose Hall (www.whitewitchgolf.com), the Cinnamon Hill course at the Hilton Rose Hall Resort (www.resortsbyhilton.com) and Spa and Ironshore Golf and Country Club, all created by internationally acclaimed designers and offering a challenge for all ability levels. These courses are open to the public.

Walking, Hiking and Cycling

Jamaica is a perfect island for walking, hiking or mountain biking, and more and more visitors are looking to get off the beaten track, at least for part of their holiday.

A guide is recommended for a trek to the Blue Mountain Peak or a hike into the Cockpit Country. Several companies organise tours that can be tailored to your needs. The

Southern Trelawny Environmental Association (STEA) provides local guides for Cockpit Country tours (tel: 393-6584; www.stea.net). Sun Venture Tours run hiking, caving, cycling, safari, sightseeing, birdwatching and adventure tours island-wide (tel: 1876-924-4515; www.sunventuretours.com). Strawberry Hill Hotel, which is located in Blue Mountains (www.strawberryhillhotel.com), has several guided hikes of different difficulty levels. For mountain biking on footpaths and goat trails, check Blue Mountain Bicycle Tours (tel: 974-7075; www.bmtoursja.com). Blue Mountain Bicycle Tours also organises guided cycling trips down the 460m (1,500ft) drop from Murphy Hill to Dunn's River Falls (see also Bicycle Rental, page 116).

For news and information about competitive cycling meets, charity rides and racing, contact the Jamaica Cycling Federation (www.jamaicacycling.com).

Horse Riding

There are several places in Jamaica to get in the saddle. Try the facilities at the Rocky Point Stables at the Half Moon Hotel (tel: 953-2286; www.horsebackridingjamaica.com); or Braco Stables, Duncans, Trelawny, 15 minutes' drive from Falmouth (tel: 954-0185; www.bracostables.com), which offers a variety of rides and tours.

See the island on horseback

Cricket on the green

SPECTATOR SPORTS

Spectator sports tend to be seasonal. Depending on the time of year, you can attend a range of competitive events.

Cricket

The professional season in Jamaica runs from January to August each year (Jamaica Cricket Association; www.cricketjamaica.org) and international matches are usually played at Sabina Park, Kingston. You might also come across a local game in almost any village. The English introduced cricket to the island, but Jamaican players and spectators bow to nobody in their obvious enthusiasm for the game.

Soccer

Soccer is hugely popular on Jamaica. The season runs from September to May; the premier league has 12 sides (www.premierleaguejamaica.com) and there are 13 parish leagues. The national squad is known as the Reggae Boyz (www.thereggaeboyz.com). Jamaica last qualified for the World Cup in 1998.

Horse Racing

There is a track at Caymanas Park near Kingston (www.caymanasracetrack.com). Betting is in Jamaican dollars only.

Polo

Matches are played at several places but you can watch an international match at Kingston Polo Club , St Ann Polo Club, Drax Hall (www.stannspoloclub.com) and at Chukka Cove near St Ann's Bay in the north. The polo season runs from January to early August. The Jamaica Polo Association is based at St Ann Polo Club, Drax Hall, St Ann, near Ocho Rios.

NIGHTLIFE AND ENTERTAINMENT

Jamaicans love to listen (and dance) to local music. Reggae has been a huge influence on pop music throughout the world. Jamaica has one of the world's most intense grassroots music traditions with a competitive, lucrative recording industry.

You'll find live music in bars and restaurants every night. These will be advertised in the free tourist magazines in your hotel, or out on the street booming from speakers on tops of cars. Negril, Ocho Rios and Montego Bay all have nightclubs that stay open very late.

Having a ball in Margaritaville, Montego Bay

Many hotels have Jamaican nights where you can watch a dance show and do some dancing yourself. These traditional evenings often feature the rhythms of the

Dance to some traditional beats

wider Caribbean, such as calypso (Trinidad) and merengue (Dominican Republic).

The island's biggest music festival is 'Reggae Sumfest' (www.reggaesumfest.com), which is held at a variety of venues in Montego Bay each July and features local and international artists. Ocho Rios also has an annual jazz festival in June (www.ochoriosjazz.com). For a full calendar see www.visitjamaica.com.

SHOPPING

One thing that you notice about Jamaica is that many shops come to you. You won't be able to walk down the street without someone approaching you with crafts and other commodities. Buying from the street traders means there is no set price, and some people feel uncomfortable about haggling. Bargaining is supposed to be an enjoyable interaction, and nobody can make you buy something that you don't want (see page 64).

The major resort towns all have duty-free shopping centres with a range of jewellery, perfume, leather goods and other quality products from around the world. Some of these items can be purchased with savings of up to 30 percent on prices back home, but not everything offers such good value.

ARTS AND CRAFTS

Wood carving. The Jamaican people are highly skilled in the art of carving wood. It is one aspect of communal pride that has carried on since colonial times. Woodcarvings are a major souvenir product, and there is a huge range from fine carved pieces to objects in the rough 'naive' style.

You will see natural wood and also a range of colourful productions in the red, yellow and green Rasta colours. Different types of wood have different weights and different finishes. Some of the pieces are extremely lightweight, but the dark lignum vitae wood is heavy and has a beautiful finish when carved. Don't buy articles if the wood still looks green: it has not been allowed to season properly and will split as it dries.

Jewellery. There is also an amazing range of jewellery made from local products and semiprecious stones, but you should be aware that some of the materials used are from protected species. Both tortoiseshell and coral are still on sale. Don't buy them. Not only is it illegal to import these articles back into your home country, but it encourages traders to take more of these endangered living creatures from the sea. Some traders will tell you that the coral jewellery or tortoiseshell they are selling was not taken from the sea but was washed up on the beaches; this is just a sales ploy.

Basket weaving. You will also find a wide variety of basket ware made locally from the rushes that can be found in huge beds all around the island. The dried-rush baskets are still used in many households today, and they make a very practical souvenir of your visit to Jamaica.

Art and ceramics. If you want to spend a bit more money on handcrafted goods, there are a number of galleries around the island where you can buy paintings and ceramics by some of the leading artists in Jamaica and the wider Caribbean. The Half Moon Shopping Centre (just east of Montego Bay) has a gallery. To see crafts being made, tour the studios of the Wassi Art Pottery Factory, near Ocho Rios.

CLOTHING

Cool clothing remains a popular choice for shoppers, and Jamaica offers a wide range from designer wear in the boutiques of Kingston to the practical batik sarongs and T-shirts sold in beach stalls. Look out for the 'Reggae to Wear' range.

Jamaican rum packs a punch

COFFEE

Blue Mountain coffee can be bought and taken home in a number of forms. The roasted beans are sold in small sacks or in vacuum-packed foil containers. The beans can also be ground and then packed in tins or foil packs. Presentation packs (pretty printed bags) add an attractive exterior to the delicious contents. You can buy direct from the growers after a farm tour and a tasting. Worth a visit is the Old Tavern Coffee Estate (tel: 924-2785) run by the Twyman family in Green Hills, Portland, where an informative tour is provided. Remember that High Mountain coffee is not of the same quality as Blue Mountain coffee.

RUM

The drink that sustained a thousand pirates and generations of local people, Jamaican rum is said to be the best in the Caribbean – although other islands may beg to differ. Try before you buy. Appleton Distillery (tel: 963-9216, www.appletonestate.com) in St Elizabeth offers a free tasting session as part of its tour, including some mixed-rum drinks that are less alcoholic but equally delicious (see page 106). All these products are available throughout the island and at duty-free shops in the airport.

CIGARS

For over 40 years, Jamaica has had a small-scale industry that produces a range of well-regarded cigars. These can be bought duty-free to take home with you. However, Cuban cigars are also a major business here. Jamaica is only 145km (90 miles) from the south coast of Cuba and imports a full range of what are reputed to be the finest cigars in the world, though they cannot be brought legally back to the USA.

CHILDREN'S JAMAICA

Jamaica is an ideal island for children of all ages. Kids can play for hours at the beach building sandcastles, swimming, or simply splashing in the water. Seven Mile Beach (Long Bay) at Negril is perfect for young children, but all the major resorts have clean, safe beaches with good facilities. Older children will enjoy snorkelling, scuba diving or taking a ride on a glass-bottomed boat. Take a trip underwater in a semi-submersible boat at Montego Bay and your children will be captivated by the sea life that lies so close to the shore. Also at Montego Bay is the **Aquasol Theme Park** offering a whole host of water sports activities.

Adventurous kids will enjoy a cruise up Black River into the Great Morass Mangrove Swamp to meet crocodiles, which come so close you can almost shake hands with them. At Dunn's River Falls there's excitement for children and adults alike, plus lots of water activities. For a more relaxing kind of fun try floating down the Martha Brae River on a raft.

Negril is the perfect place for children

Most large hotel complexes have children's clubs where kids can spend the whole day enjoying activities and excursions. Conversely, some hotels on Jamaica operate on an 'adults-only' policy.

Cover every inch of young skin with a high factor sun cream, limit kids' time in the sun for the first few days of your holiday and always keep them out of the midday sun. Also make sure that they are well supervised whenever they are near the water.

FESTIVALS AND EVENTS

Exact dates vary. If you want to attend a particular event, check with the Jamaica Tourist Board (www.visitjamaica.com). Easter time in Jamaica is the start of carnival main events in Kingston, Negril and Montego Bay.

January *Rebel Salute* music festival; Negril Sprint Triathlon (Long Bay); *Air Jamaica Jazz & Blues Festival* (Montego Bay).

6 January *Accompong Maroon Festival*.

6 February *Bob Marley Birthday Bash*.

February *Pineapple Cup Yacht Race* (Miami to Montego Bay); Fi Wi Sinting (African heritage festival, Portland).

March *Stepping High Festival* (Negril).

April Montego Bay Yacht Club Easter Regatta.

June *Ocho Rios Jazz Festival; Kingston on the Edge Art Festival*.

July *International Reggae Day Festival* (Kingston); *Portland Jerk Festival*; *Reggae Sumfest* (international music festival, Montego Bay); *Little Ochi Seafood Festival* (Alligator Pond, Mandeville); Seville Emancipation Jubilee (heritage festival, St Ann's Bay).

August *Mello Go Roun'* (festival of performing arts, Kingston). Ocho Rios Seafood Festival (Ocho Rios); Breadfruit Festival (Bath, St Ann).

6 August *Independence Day Parade* (street carnival featuring *Junkanoo* dancers, Kingston/island wide).

September Falmouth Blue Marlin Tournament.

October Port Antonio International Marlin Tournament (see page 89) and Port Antonio Local Canoe Tournament; National Heroes Day (island wide); Africa Jamfest (Montego Bay).

November Rastafari Rootzfest; NyamJam Food and Music Festival.

December *Reggae Marathon and Half Marathon* (Negril); *Jonkonnu* (also known as Junkanoo; street parades and Christmas celebrations across the island); JMMC *All Stages Rally Jamaica* (motorsports race, Kingston); Milk River Seafood and Jerk Festival.

EATING OUT

Jamaica is a large and fertile island. Fruits and vegetables grow in abundance on family farms, and the land is grazed by cattle, goats and pigs. The clear waters are full of edible fish as well as lobster, shrimp and other seafood. You will be offered an amazing variety of dishes, all very fresh. The range of eating opportunities across the island is remarkable, from cheap street stalls and beach bars to fine restaurants offering international and 'new Jamaican' cooking.

WHAT TO EAT

The island's historical and ethnic heritage has contributed to a unique cuisine: it is a story of African cooking techniques and Indian spices meeting Caribbean ingredients. Jamaican food has a reputation for being spicy but, surprisingly, most of the dishes are tasty but not hot. The heat comes from a sauce found in a little bottle that is always on the table, allowing you to add as much spice as you like – or none at all. This hot sauce is manufactured on the island with a secret recipe based on 'Scotch bonnet' pepper, one of the hottest in the world. A little goes a long way, so start carefully and discover your personal taste level.

You will find tame versions of all Jamaican dishes on the menu at large hotels, which often provide a night of Jamaican cuisine where you can sample a range of dishes along with some Jamaican entertainment.

Jamaican Cuisine

Ackee and saltfish. This dish was once a staple food for the enslaved Africans who were transported to the island, and it is now the official national dish of Jamaica. *Ackee*, which is native to Ghana in West Africa, is a vegetable now found in great abundance on Jamaica. The ackee is harvested only when it is ripe, as it is poisonous otherwise. It is chopped and cooked until it takes on the appearance of firm scrambled eggs. The enslaved Africans added a small amount of protein-rich salted codfish for a cheap and nutritious way to start the day. Today ackee is often served with other types of fish or with bacon as part of a traditional Jamaican breakfast. It comes with various kinds of carbohydrate such as dumplings called 'Johnny cakes', or perhaps with *bammy*, a cassava pancake.

Ackee, fresh from the tree

Meat dishes. Jamaicans always cook their meat well rather than rare, so you won't have to worry about the dangers of under-cooked meat. But meat served in local restaurants is chopped into pieces with a cleaver rather than being butchered and trimmed, so beware of sharp pieces of bone which might be present in the prepared dish.

Jerk. The modern national dish of Jamaica is 'jerk', which takes its name from the hot marinade used to season meats or fish. You will find it everywhere from the menus of fine restaurants to beach bars and street barbecue stalls. The dish was invented in Maroon country (near Boston Bay in the east of the island) and was originally used to tenderise pork, which was then cooked slowly and served hot and tender. The marinade became popular across the island for all meat, and today you can eat jerk chicken and even jerk fish. The Boston recipe is a mixture of 21 spices and very piquant indeed.

You can watch jerk pork and chicken being prepared in Boston Bay and then try it for yourself. The meat is freshly butchered (the animals are slaughtered in the mornings under the auspices of health inspectors), then marinated and cooked within hours. You will be served the meat with breadfruit, which has a neutral flavour to cool the palate. In other parts of the island, the jerk ranges in flavour and hotness. In hotels and international restaurants, it can be quite mild; you'll find that Jamaicans snub their noses at such offerings.

Goat curry. There are herds of goats alongside all the highways and byways of Jamaica. Goat curry (referred to as 'curry goat') became part of the Jamaican diet following the arrival of the Indian itinerant workers who came to work the plantations following the abolition of slavery. The curry style has adapted over the generations and is now really more of a flavour than a true Indian method of preparation.

Fish dishes. A most amazing array of fish and shellfish can be found in the waters surrounding Jamaica. You can be guaranteed absolutely fresh seafood because the small boats come in daily with their catch. In many restaurants the 'catch of the day' will be the tastiest and freshest option. It might be tuna, snapper, or kingfish; whatever the choice, it will always be superb. The

Full of flavour

Authentic Jamaican cuisine is flavoursome thanks to the spices and seasonings used to marinate the meat and fish, usually overnight. They can include pimento, allspice, thyme, garlic, cloves, ginger and fiery scotch bonnet (peppers).

Jerk chicken with black beans

lobster and conch are also fresh and delicious, although they are seasonal. Different areas of the island specialise in certain types of seafood. Around Bluefields, south of Negril, it is spicy shrimp, and at Middle Quarter you will find Escoveitch fish (similar to ceviche), which is fried and then pickled.

Rice and peas. Most main dishes are accompanied by a side dish of rice and peas. It originated as an inexpensive and nutritious option in colonial times, when it could be served as a meal in itself when money was scarce. The 'peas' (actually red or kidney beans) and the rice are cooked slowly together with a touch of coconut milk.

Vegetables and fruit. Because fresh vegetables in Jamaica are varied and plentiful, you will always be given a generous accompaniment with any main dish. The list includes *callaloo* (a spinach-like vegetable), yam, breadfruit, pumpkin and potatoes. Starchy vegetables have been a staple of Jamaican diets since the days

Fresh fruit and vegetables in Spanish Town

of slavery when they were needed to provide energy for hard labour.

You can sample the abundant fresh fruits from stalls in the street or from hawkers on the beach. Hotels will have a wonderful selection at breakfast or to finish a meal in the evening. Bananas are obviously popular, but you can also choose from guava, mango, papaya, pineapple and coconut. There is in addition a range of unusual fruits found only in Jamaica. Look out for sweetsop and soursop (rough-skinned fruits, said to be aphrodisiacs and best made into a milky drink) along with the star apple and the *ugli* (a citrus fruit).

As one of the island's major crops, the banana has a special place in Jamaican cuisine. It is eaten raw but also in many hot desserts. You can have banana fritters and, for a touch of luxury, bananas flambéed in Jamaican rum.

Other hot and cold desserts include tarts and custard, which is traditionally flavoured with coconut cream. Ice creams made with fresh fruit are also extremely refreshing: 'matrimony' is a Jamaican favourite, which mixes orange and star apples with cream. Other local favourites include rum and raisin and grapenut ice cream.

Snacks. Jamaican fast food consists of a number of cheap dishes that are prepared at home or bought at roadside stalls for lunch on the run. 'Patties' are thin oven-baked pastries filled with meat, fish or vegetables. 'Stamp-and-go' are fish fritters, so called because just before being cooked they are flattened with the palm of the hand. These dishes are often served as hors d'oeuvres in hotels or in private homes.

International Cuisine

In addition to serving toned-down versions of local dishes, Jamaica's resorts offer a wide range of international cuisine. There are a number of Italian restaurants all across the island, from those offering quick trattoria-style service to upscale dining establishments with full service. Visitors seeking Mexican and Chinese cooking will find choices as well, and the comforts of American and Continental food are also available. There are branches of international fast-food chains in Kingston, Montego Bay and Ocho Rios if you want a burger or fried chicken.

WHAT TO DRINK

One advantage of a trip to Jamaica is that you can drink the tap water. You can be assured that food washed in tap water is safe to eat and that ice made from it is safe in your sodas or frozen daiquiris.

Beer. Red Stripe, a lager-type beer, has long been associated with Jamaica. It is light and very refreshing on a long, hot Jamaican day. You will find it in every café and bar. However, Jamaicans also have a liking for stout beers, which they like to drink at room temperature. You will find that Dragon Stout and

Red Stripe

You might hear some older locals asking for a 'policeman' at the bar. Don't be alarmed – they just want a Red Stripe beer. The name was taken from the stripes on the trousers and cap of the Jamaican police uniform.

Appleton rum

Guinness are widely available. You can order your drink cold if you don't mind the locals having a little joke at your expense.

Rum. The first thing that you will be offered when you arrive at your hotel is a rum cocktail. Appleton, the 'overproof' white rum, is the best-known brand, used as the basis for almost limitless recipes. Whichever rum you choose, be careful because they all pack a punch. Many hotels and bars will have their own special recipes, but most will combine rum with fresh fruit juice, lime, or coconut milk. Rum can also be combined with cream and other flavourings to produce a range of smooth after-dinner drinks. Perhaps the best known liqueur is Tia Maria (produced from the Jamaican coffee bean), which makes the perfect accompaniment to a hot cup of coffee.

Non-alcoholic drinks. The choice of fruit juices is huge, and you can find single juices or blends in every bar and restaurant. 'Ting', a refreshing fizzy grapefruit drink, is locally-produced. Jamaica also produces a ginger ale which has a little more kick than the standard and is extremely refreshing in the heat of the day. You will find all the internationally recognised brands of fizzy drinks readily available.

Cocoa. Jamaican cocoa beans contain a chemical which is a mild stimulant. The roasted and ground beans or seeds can be used to make a delicious hot drink as well as chocolate.

Jamaican coffee. Said to be the best in the world and extremely expensive due to the small crop and high demand, most Blue Mountain coffee is exported, so you might not find it in every establishment on the island. The coffee is extremely mild and low in caffeine, with a hint of natural sweetness.

During the 1960s, the reputation of Blue Mountain coffee suffered because inferior lowland beans began to be blended with quality mountain beans to increase the crop and meet demand. In 1973, the government stepped in to create an official standard for Blue Mountain coffee, thus restoring confidence in the marketplace. Today, only coffee grown at an altitude of 610m (2,000ft) or above can be sold as 100 percent Blue Mountain. You might also discover products advertised as 'blended' Blue Mountain coffee; these will contain at least 20 percent Blue Mountain beans.

A cocoa pod containing the seeds that make chocolate

PLACES TO EAT

We have used the following symbols to give an idea of the price for a three-course meal for one, excluding drinks; tips are extra. Prices are in US dollars:

$$$$	over $50
$$$	$30–50
$$	$20–30
$	below $20

MONTEGO BAY

Houseboat Grill $$–$$$$ *Southern Cross Boulevard, Montego Bay, tel: 979-8845*, www.thehouseboatgrill.com. Restaurant on a houseboat moored in the Marine Park. Dinner only, with the bar open from 4.30pm for sunset drinks. Fusion cuisine, offering meat and seafood and some excellent vegetarian options. A glass-bottomed section is fascinating for children. Daily 6–11pm.

Margaritaville $–$$ *Gloucester Avenue, Montego Bay, tel: 952-4777*, www.margaritavillecaribbean.com. Lively sports bar and grill located at the start of the main strip. Roof-top deck with water chute and floating trampoline. Frequent 'special' evenings with themed entertainment. More formal (and more expensive) dining at Marguerite's next door. Also in Ocho Rios and Negril. Daily 10–4am

MVP Smokehouse $–$$ *Bogue Road, Reading St. James, Montego Bay, tel: 622-7198.*This popular, authentic Jamaican restaurant on the outskirts of Montego Bay serves excellent jerk chicken, pork, fish, shrimp and lobster that can be accompanied by signature sauces, sweet potatoes, rice and bammy. Tue–Thu 11.30am–9pm, Fri–Sun until 10pm.

Pier 1 $$$ *Howard Cooke Boulevard, Montego Bay, tel: 952-2452*, www.pier1jamaica.com. Picturesquely located on the waterfront, Pier 1 is an open-air seafood restaurant that turns into a vibrant nightclub after 10pm. The menu features sandwiches, wraps, soups as well as some Jamaican-style specials. Daily 11am–11pm.

The Pelican Grill $$–$$$ *Gloucester Avenue, Montego Bay, tel: 952-3171,* www.pelicangrillja.com. Long established local favourite that is popular with visitors too. Hearty Jamaican food, including a good breakfast menu, and American specialities. Good value for money and has free pick-up from most larger hotels in Montego Bay. Daily 7am–10pm.

The Pork Pit $ *27 Gloucester Avenue, Montego Bay, tel: 952-1046.* Very basic, but very good Jamaican food – jerk chicken, pork and ribs sold by weight, served through the kitchen window, with garden gazebos to sit and eat in. Cash only. Sun–Thu 11am–11pm, Fri–Sat 11am–midnight.

Scotchie's $ *Falmouth Road, Montego Bay, tel: 953-8041.* Casual dining near Rose Hall and the Holiday Inn, serving some of the best jerk pork, chicken and fish. Also has branches in Ocho Rios, Scotchie's Too (near St Ann's Polo Club) and in Kingston, Scotchie's Jerk Center (2 Chelsea Avenue). Daily 11am–11pm.

FALMOUTH

Glistening Waters $$–$$$ *Luminous Lagoon, Rock, tel: 954-3229,* www.glisteningwaters.com. Before your meal, take a boat trip at night on the bioluminescent lagoon, or swim in the water for an explosive experience. Good seafood and international as well as Jamaican dishes. Daily 11am–10pm, bar until 1am.

RUNAWAY BAY

Ultimate Jerk Centre $ *Main Street, Discovery Bay, tel: 973-2054.* A casual, popular roadside restaurant serving tasty, affordable and authentic Jamaican food. Every Friday night there is a happy hour and music, last Saturday of the month is an Old Hits party with local DJ. They also hold a New Year's Eve party here. Sun–Thu 9am–10pm, Fri–Sat 9am–11.30pm.

OCHO RIOS

Almond Tree $$$$ *Hibiscus Lodge Hotel, Main Street, Ocho Rios, tel: 974-2676.* A hotel restaurant offering great views of the sea and serving international and local cuisine. Inside and open-air dining by candlelight. Live music three nights a week, piano bar. Also excellent Jamaican breakfast. Daily 7.30–10.30am, noon–3pm, 6–9.30pm.

Evita's Italian Restaurant $$–$$$$ *Eden Bower Road, Ocho Rios, tel: 974-2333,* www.evitasjamaica.com. Italian food with a touch of Jamaican spice; house specialities are Lasagna Rastafari, One Love Penne and Jerk Spaghetti. Try the Jamaica Bobsled for dessert. The essential place to see-and-be-seen. Daily 11am–11pm.

Juici Patties $ *1 Newlin Street, Ocho Rios.* If you love patties, this small fast-food place (part of a chain in Jamaica) cooks up some of the best on the island. The fillings include beef, chicken, shrimp, lobster, soy and cheese. Be prepared to queue. Mon–Sat 8am–7pm.

PORT ANTONIO

Anna Banana's $$ *7 Folly Road, Port Antonio, tel: 715-6533.* A small beach-side restaurant and sports bar located a little way out of the town centre. Decent Jamaican cuisine, with seafood specialities and good value for money. Daily 8am–11pm

Dickie's Best Kept Secret $$$–$$$$ *Port Antonio western outskirts, tel: 809-6276.* An unassuming painted shack on a clifftop overlooking the bay, run by Dickie Butler, who is rumoured to have entertained Errol Flynn, Princess Margaret and Winnie Mandela, among others. Reservations recommended. Mon–Thu 9am–7pm, Fri–Sat until 8.30pm

Mille Fleurs $$$ *Hotel Mocking Bird Hill, Port Antonio, tel: 993-7134,* www.hotelmockingbirdhill.com. A creative mix of international and local cuisine. Locally-grown produce, with some from the restaurant's own organic garden. Located in a beautiful position in the foothills of the Blue Mountains offering spectacular views. If you are not a guest in the hotel, you need to reserve 24 hours in advance. Daily 8–10am, noon–2pm, 7–9pm

BLUE MOUNTAINS

The Gap Café $$-$$$ *Hardware Gap, Newcastle, tel: 361-4192,* www.thegapjm.com. High up in the hills with views over Kingston, this renovated 19th-century way station is an ideal place to stop when hiking or touring the Blue Mountains. Jamaican and Italian food, from curry goat to pizza. Daily 10am until 6pm, Fri–Sun until 7pm.

KINGSTON

Usain Bolt's Tracks and Records $$ *67 Constant Spring Road, Kingston 10 Market Place, tel: 926-7875,* www.tracksandrecords.com. Owned by 8-gold medal Olympian, Usain Bolt, this popular sports bar-style restaurant serves traditional Jamaican dishes and other international food. Branches are also found in Ocho Rios and Montego Bay. Daily 11.30am–12am.

Jade Garden $$$ *Shops 54–59, Sovereign Centre, 106 Hope Road, Kingston, tel: 978-3476,* Hong Kong chefs prepare traditional Chinese food and the island's two largest saltwater tanks ensure that all seafood is absolutely fresh. Views of the Blue Mountains from picture windows are spectacular. Reservations recommended. Open daily noon–10pm, Sun from 11am–9pm.

Regency Bar & Lounge $$$-$$$$ *Terra Nova All-Suite Hotel, 17 Waterloo Road, Kingston, tel: 926-2211,* www.terranovajamaica.com. One of the best restaurants in town, serving international cuisine with a Caribbean twist. Good seafood and extensive wine list. Formal dress code. Open daily: bar 11am–1am, restaurant 6.30–10.30pm.

Tamarind Indian Cuisine $$ *28 Orchard Village Plaza, 18-22 Barbican Road, Kingston, tel: 977-0695,* www.tamarindindiancuisine.com. Hearty Indian and Asian fusion dishes in the vicinity of the Bob Marley Museum. The selection is great, the food delicious and the portions are generous - the only downside is that it is often packed. Mon–Fri 11.30am–4pm & 5.30–9.30pm, Sat 11.30am–10pm and Sun 1.00–9.30pm.

TREASURE BEACH (SOUTH COAST)

Jack Sprat $-$$$ *Treasure Beach, tel: 965-3000, 491-0649*, www.jakeshotel.com Great beach bar at the western end of Jakes (see page 139). Typical wooden shack with music, bar, pizzas, ice cream, catch of the day and lots of specials, such as lobster curry when in season. Daily 10am–10pm.

Jakes $$-$$$$ *Jakes Hotel, Calabash Bay, Treasure Beach, tel: 965-3000*, www.jakeshotel.com. The best of Jamaica's spicy cuisine, including saltfish and ackee, rice and peas, fish in coconut milk and Escoveitch fish. The catch is always fresh, the vegetables and fruit local. Soups include conch chowder and cream of pumpkin. Daily 10am–10pm.

Little Ochie $-$$ *Alligator Pond Beach, tel: 852-6430*. Great setting on the beach with wooden tables under thatch, some made from old fishing boats on stilts. Choose your own fish, lobster or other seafood, have it cooked to order and served with bammy, festival and scotch bonnet chillies (these can be very hot). Daily 8.30am–midnight.

Yabba $$$ *Treasure Beach Hotel, Treasure Beach, tel: 965-0110*, www.jamaicatreasurebeachhotel.com. Jamaican and international cuisine, including fresh seafood, served in a relaxing atmosphere. The vegetables are grown on the owner's farm. Daily 7am–10pm.

NEGRIL

Ivan's Bar and Restaurant $$-$$$$ *West End Road, Negril, tel: 957-0390*, www.catchajamaica.com. Restaurant at the Catcha Falling Star Hotel, lovely location on the cliffs overlooking the water with a romantic vibe. Get there at 6pm for the sunset. Daily 5–11pm.

Just Natural Restaurant $$ *West End Road, Negril, tel: 957-0235*. Excellent vegetarian meals from appetizers to desserts. Also offers fresh fish and seafood. Particularly good for authentic Jamaican breakfast with a huge fruit plate and Blue Mountain coffee. Daily 8am–9pm.

Margaritaville Bar and Grill $$-$$$ *Norman Manley Boulevard, Negril, tel: 957-4467,* www.margaritavillecaribbean.com. Lively sports bar and grill located centrally on Negril's beach. Convenient for lounging on the beach, with full service available. Frequent 'special' evenings with themed entertainment. Free pick-up service. Daily 10–4am

Niah's Patties $ *Seven Mile Beach, Negril.* At the back of the craft market stalls just off the beach, this little shack serves up authentic hand-made patties to fill a hole at any time of the day. Several varieties are offered, from lobster to vegetable, all with accompanying sauces. Daily 10am–8pm.

Norma's on the Beach $$$ *Sea Splash Resort, Negril, tel: 957-4041.* Restaurant on a deck overlooking the water with a romantic atmosphere. European cuisine with a Jamaican nouvelle flair by local chef, Norma Shirley. Open for breakfast, lunch and dinner. Daily 9am–5pm.

Presley's Bar & Grill $$$$ *West End Road, Negril, tel: 440-9833.* Informal, local place offering fresh local seafood and produce. Really tasty food and huge portions. Dinner is by reservation only, so book the day before. Only four tables in Presley's shack tucked in between stalls, across the road from Rockhouse Hotel. Daily noon–midnight.

Rick's Café $$-$$$$ *West End Road, Negril, tel: 957-0380,* www.rickscafejamaica.com. Offering everything from surf 'n' turf to chip 'n' dips. The place to come for sunset watching. Live music during the evenings; a lively, happening place. Daily noon–9.30pm.

Treehouse Restaurant $$$$ *Norman Manley Boulevard, Negril,* tel: 957-4287, http://negriltreehouse.net. Imaginative Jamaican cuisine. Have chicken, pork, fish and seafood cooked any way you like, as well as pizza. There is jazz on Sundays and breakfast on the beach. Daily 8am–11pm.

Xtabi Cliff Restaurant $$-$$$ *Xtabi Resort, Lighthouse Road, Negril, tel: 957- 0524,* www.xtabinegril.com. This place is justly proud of its lobster and meat dishes, chargrilled or cooked any way you like. Daily 8am–11pm.

A–Z TRAVEL TIPS

A SUMMARY OF PRACTICAL INFORMATION

A Accommodation 115
Airports 115
B Bicycle Rental 116
Budgeting for Your Trip 117
C Car hire 118
Climate 119
Clothing 120
Crime and Safety 120
D Driving 121
E Electricity 122
Embassies and Consulates 122
Emergencies 123
G Getting There 123
Guides and Tours 124
H Health and Medical Care 124
L Language 125
LGBTQ Travellers 125
M Media 125
Money 126
O Opening times 127
P Police 127
Post Offices 127
Public Holidays 128
R Religion 128
T Telephones 128
Time Zones 129
Tipping 129
Tourist Information 129
Transport 130
V Visas and Entry Requirements 131
W Websites and Internet Access 131
Y Youth Hostels 131

A

ACCOMMODATION

Jamaica has a full range of accommodation, from basic beach shacks to some of the finest resorts in the Caribbean and small family-run hotels can be found both close to the beach and inland in the mountains. In Kingston the best hotels are designed for business travellers, while guest houses are of variable quality and not particularly cheap.

All-inclusive resorts were invented in Jamaica and are found mostly along the north and west coasts. Some hotels accept couples only and others cater for families, but most offer a wide range of sporting activities, wedding and honeymoon packages and excursions.

There are also some boutique hotels where you can be pampered in luxury and enjoy some of the island's most beautiful scenery on the coast and in the mountains. These do not come cheap. Many of the small luxury hotels have been around since the 1950s, attracting movie stars and the glitterati before mass tourism arrived, this includes the Island Outpost group.

Jamaica also has a wide range of private villas for rent, with or without staff. Contact the Jamaica Association of Villas and Apartments (JAVA), Office #4, Ocean Village Shopping Centre, Ocho Rios, St Ann (tel: 452-1268, www.javavillas.org) for more details.

For general information on rental of cabins in the Blue Mountains, contact the Jamaica Conservation and Development Trust, the local NGO responsible for the management of the Blue and John Crow Mountains National Park (tel: 920-8278/9, www.jcdt.org.jm).

Prices change dramatically between high and low season. Low season is from mid-April to mid-December, and you can make savings of up to 40 percent during this period. High season is extremely busy, so it is important to make reservations well in advance to guarantee the accommodation of your choice.

AIRPORTS (see also Getting There)

There are three international airports.

Norman Manley International Airport at Kingston (KIN; tel: 924-8452-6; www.nmia.aero), serves Kingston and the east of the island; it also caters to international business travellers. Transfer to Kingston takes 20 minutes and is 15km (9.5 miles). There is a bus service, but a taxi direct to your destination is a more sensible option. Transfer time to Port Antonio is around three hours.

Sangster International Airport at Montego Bay (MBJ; tel: 952-3124; www.mbjairport.com), serves the north coast, the west of the island and also handles the charter aircraft that fly to the island. Central Montego Bay is only 5 minutes away and there are taxis outside the terminal building even though many hotels and resorts provide transport for the short transfer. Transfers to other resorts by coach are as follows: Ocho Rios is around 2 hours, Runaway Bay 1.5 hours and Negril one hour.

Ian Fleming International Airport (OCJ; tel: 975-3101; www.ifia.aero) near Ocho Rios, opened in 2011 and serves specialised small charters and private jets up to the size of a Dash 8.

There are also a number of domestic airports: Negril Aerodrome, Ken Jones Airport (Port Antonio) and Tinson Pen (Kingston), which operate transfer flights from the international airports. In Kingston, most domestic flights leave from Tinson Pen.

B

BICYCLE RENTAL

Bicycle rental is a sensible way to see a little more of the area where you are based. It is particularly useful in Negril, where the land is flat. Contact Dependable Bike Rental (tel: 957-4764), in Negril, or Kool Bike Rental (http://koolbikerental.tripod.com) at the Negril Yacht Club for bicycles or motorbikes. Cycles can be rented by the day or by the week. It is also possible to undertake bicycle tours into the Blue Mountains and around Port Antonio, along the relatively quiet roads (see page 91).

BUDGETING FOR YOUR TRIP

To help you budget for your trip, here are some prices for the things you will need.

Flights to Jamaica. A charter flight from London in the UK to Montego Bay starts from about £400 including taxes, while a scheduled flight to either Kingston or Montego Bay starts from around £500. These are low season prices and fluctuations occur throughout the year. From the US, the best deals are from Florida, with return tickets on budget airlines, such as Jet Blue, starting from about US$160 excluding tax.

Accommodation. A room can range in price from US$45 in low season for a hideaway such as Ital Rest Cottages (see page 139) to US$1,800 per night for a suite in a top-class hotel such as Jamaica Inn (see page 135) in high season, depending on whether you opt for room only (EP) or for a fully inclusive luxury resort hotel (AI). For a room in a less expensive hotel, allow US$45–100 per person; for a medium-standard hotel, prices range from US$100–250 per night. All-inclusive resorts and luxury hotels start at over US$200 per day but can rise to more than US$1,000, depending on the facilities and comfort level provided.

Self catering. Rental rates of houses, cottages and studios in resorts start from US$500 per week, but for a villa with fully fitted kitchen and maid service expect to pay over US$1,500 per week, and for the very luxurious (such as those at Blue Lagoon), from US$7,500 per week. These prices can prove to be good value on a per-person basis.

Meals. For lunch in a moderately priced but good establishment allow US$20 per person plus drinks; for dinner, allow US$40 per person plus drinks.

Car rental. Allow around US$32–120 per day depending on the size of car and whether the hire company is local or international. The lower figure is the price for a compact car from a local company in low season, while the higher price is for a compact 4x4 from an international company. Weekly rates are better value. If you want to hire a car with a driver, expect to pay around US$100–180, depending on distance, for a 10-hour day, including fuel.

Local transport. Bus fares are cheap, both in town and for longer distances,

if you have the stomach for a journey at speed, often on twisting mountain roads. In Kingston the urban bus fare is US$1 and express buses US$2.50–2.75. However, travelling by bus is not recommended for the fainthearted. Taxis charge about US$5 for a short journey and US$20 for 10 miles, but check the fare beforehand. For long journeys the taxi fare could be more than hiring a car, but you can negotiate a deal with a small taxi company.
Arriving and Departing. An air arrival tax of $20 in addition to an arrival tax of $20 and a departure tax of $35 are usually included in the price of your flight ticket.

C

CAR HIRE

Jamaica is the third-largest of the Caribbean islands, and to see all its delights it is best to hire private transport. The condition of the roads and Jamaican driving habits do create concerns for car hirers (see Driving), but with common sense and care, renting a car should enhance your trip, not spoil it.

The major car rental companies have offices at the two international airports:

Hertz: Kingston (tel: 924-8028, at the airport), www.hertz.com.
Avis: Kingston (tel: 924-8293, at the airport), Montego Bay (tel: 952-0762, at the airport), www.avis.com.jm.
Island Car Rentals is the largest local fleet: Kingston (tel: 926-5875, and at the airport, tel: 924-8075), Montego Bay (tel: 952-7225, at the airport), www.islandcarrentals.com, minimum age 23.

Local companies are more competitively priced than the international companies and provide a similar quality of service. Always satisfy yourself as to the age and condition of the car before confirming the booking. You can specify whether you want a manual or automatic transmission. Many companies make an extra charge for delivering the car to your hotel; this can amount to another day's rental charge.

All national driving licences will be recognised by rental companies.

Drivers must have held a licence for at least one year before they can rent. All renters must give a deposit, which ranges from US$500 to US$1,000; if you are under 25 years of age, there will also be a bond to comply with insurance regulations. A credit card is the most sensible method of giving the deposit, although cash can also be used.

In the US, some insurance companies cover hire cars; check to see whether you are covered on your policy or through your credit card before purchasing insurance. Damage waiver is recommended, which will add around US$15 per day to your costs.

In high season it is important to book a car in advance, as demand will be high. In low season you should be able to negotiate a package that will give you a better price, and it can often be better to wait rather than book in advance.

Service stations are open daily and accept cash only (Jamaican dollars or US dollars) for fuel.

CLIMATE

Jamaica is a tropical island. It has virtually no change in seasons, the temperature varying between 25°C and 28°C (77°F and 83°F), although it is cooler in the mountains. Rainfall averages around 198cm (78in) each year and is greatest between August and November, which is considered low season for visitors. However, rain can fall in short, heavy tropical showers at all times of the year, especially in the afternoon. Rainfall varies considerably between the wetter east and the drier west of the island. Hurricane season, which afflicts the whole Caribbean, runs from the beginning of June through to the end of November.

Average daily temperatures for Jamaica:

	J	F	M	A	M	J	J	A	S	O	N	D
°C	25	25	25	26	27	28	28	28	28	27	26	25
°F	77	77	77	79	81	83	83	83	83	81	79	77

CLOTHING

Lightweight clothing is sensible throughout the year along the coasts. Many people manage happily with T-shirts and shorts during the day, and wear something a little more formal in the evening. Cotton or other breathable materials are ideal. In the mountains, sweaters are a good idea for evenings or in case of a change in the weather. If you plan to visit interior towns or Kingston, more conservative clothing might be appropriate. Beachwear is acceptable only in the immediate area of the beach and not in shops and banks.

A hat and sunglasses are important, as the sun is very strong, especially in the middle of the day. When you first arrive, always make sure that you have clothing to cover your skin to prevent burning; a lightweight long-sleeved shirt is fine.

Footwear should be light and comfortable: a pair of sandals or flip-flops for the beach, along with a smarter choice for evenings. If you plan to visit the Blue Mountains, a pair of stout shoes or walking boots is essential.

CRIME AND SAFETY

Jamaica, and Kingston in particular, have a reputation for crime and violence, but in fact there are few attacks on tourists and the Jamaican countryside has a comparatively low crime rate. Much of the violent crime is confined to about four police districts in Kingston, which are prone to drug gangs and political inter-neighbourhood rivalry. As with any city, visitors are advised to exercise caution.

The use of marijuana, or 'ganja' (as it is known on the island), is not uncommon among Jamaicans of all classes; many smoke it, while others use it as a medicinal herb. Rastafari use it as a sacrament in religious observances. The drug is easily available and most visitors will be offered a supply at some stage during their holiday. In February 2015 the parliament passed a law allowing the possession of up to 2oz (57g) for personal use.

The Jamaican authorities have increased security patrols in the resort areas, and you will see the blue uniforms of the 'Tourist Police' on the beaches. Many hotels also employ private security personnel, who patrol beaches and hotel entrances to deter hawkers and others.

Many Jamaican men make a living as impromptu (and definitely unofficial) guides, and they might approach you in the street or on the beach. Use caution in your dealings and use accredited companies only. Do not accept offers to ride in unauthorised taxis (official taxis have red number plates); they will not be insured to carry fare-paying passengers.

Always take out a travel insurance policy and photocopy important documents in case you need to make a claim.

D

DRIVING

Driving in Jamaica can be an adventure or a worry. The roads are in very bad condition and there is a lot of traffic. You might find cars driving towards you on the wrong side of the road, only to realise that they are avoiding a large pothole on their own side of the street. Always drive with utmost care and be ready to stop at any moment for potholes, animals and people. Cross-country routes, particularly in the area of the Blue Mountains, are prone to flooding or landslides. After periods of rain, you should always check before setting out to be sure that the road is passable; ask bus or truck drivers or employees at your hotel.

The North Coast Highway spans Negril–Montego Bay, Falmouth–Ocho Rios, and Ocho Rios–Port Antonio. Highway 2000 in the south connects Kingston with Montego Bay via St Catherine, Manchester, St Elizabeth, Westmoreland and Hanover, and Kingston with Ocho Rios via St Ann.

Speed limits and safety. Vehicles drive on the left, and speed limits are 50km/h (30mph) in towns and 80km/h (50mph) in rural areas. Despite this, many Jamaican drivers ignore the speed limits and drive at a dangerous speed. Always drive at a safe pace and allow plenty of time to reach your destination. Roundabouts (or traffic circles) are common. Give way to any traffic from the right at roundabouts.

Road signs feature easily recognisable international symbols. However, you will find that distance signs can be in either miles or kilometres, which can create confusion. The unit of measurement used will always be indicated at the side of the number.

Fuel and service. There are fuel stations open seven days a week in all towns. Always carry out basic checks on a rental vehicle when you take delivery of it and before setting out. Public telephones are rare in the interior; if you do break down, it could be hours before you get help, so always carry a mobile phone. If you have mechanical difficulties, contact your rental company for assistance.

Parking. When parking in towns or near beaches, try to find a car park with some security, and always park with the car in full view. At night, always park in a well-lit location.

E

ELECTRICITY

Jamaica operates at 110 volts/50 cycles as standard; current at 220 volts is available in some hotels on the island. Appliances with US and Canadian plugs can be used without adapters, but appliances from the UK and Europe will require one.

EMBASSIES AND CONSULATES

All diplomatic representatives have offices in Kingston.

Canada: High Commission, 3 West Kings House Road, Waterloo Road Entrance, Kingston 10, tel: 926-1500, www.jamaica.gc.ca

France: 13 Hillcrest Avenue, Kingston 6, tel: 619-7812, www.ambafrance-jm-bm.org.

Germany: 10 Waterloo Road, Kingston 10, tel: 926-6728, www.kingston.diplo.de.

UK: High Commission, 28 Trafalgar Road, Kingston 10, tel: 936-0700, http://ukinjamaica.fco.gov.uk/en.
US: 142 Old Hope Road, Kingston 6, tel: 702-6000, https://jm.usembassy.gov

EMERGENCIES

In the event of an emergency, call **119** for police and **110** for fire or ambulance and medical services.

G

GETTING THERE (see also Airports)

By air. Flying into Jamaica is an easy option from the US, Canada and Europe. Miami, New York, Atlanta, Chicago and Toronto are all major hubs in North America, with easy connections to other US and Canadian cities. London is the hub for Europe, with easy connections for the UK and Ireland.

The following major airlines fly into Jamaica: Air Jamaica (www.airjamaica.com), Air Canada (www.aircanada.com), American Airlines (www.aa.com), British Airways (www.britishairways.com), Delta (www.delta.com), Jet Blue (www.jetblue.com), Spirit Airlines (www.spiritair.com), and Virgin Atlantic (www.virgin-atlantic.com). Scheduled flights will normally land at Norman Manley International Airport in Kingston. If you will be spending most of your time around Montego Bay or Negril, get a flight to Sangster International Airport at Montego Bay, where the transfer time is much shorter. Many other scheduled airlines and charter companies offer services depending on the time of year, with more services during high season. Most charter flights land at Montego Bay in the north.

Visitors from Australia and New Zealand can travel through either the US or Britain to pick up a connection to Jamaica. Both directions involve long journeys and possibly a stopover en route, so consult an airline specialist for advice about schedules and costs.

By sea. Many tourists visit Jamaica as a port-of-call on a cruise. Montego Bay, Falmouth and Ocho Rios are major cruise destinations, with comprehensive facilities for cruise passengers. Ports are well placed to offer tours to a range of attractions that can be visited on a day ashore.

GUIDES AND TOURS

There is a comprehensive tour programme offering visits to sites across the island. These can be booked either through your own tour or cruise company or through the Tourist Board offices. For those who don't want to hire a car, this is an ideal way to see more of Jamaica. Tour companies will pick you up at your hotel and bring you back at the end of the day. Full-day tours often include lunch.

JUTA (Jamaican Union of Travellers Association) provides licensed taxis and tour buses for excursions to all major attractions; there are JUTA branches around the island: 80 Claude Clarke Avenue, Montego Bay, tel: 952-0813, http://jutatoursltd.com; Norman Manley Boulevard, Negril, tel: 957-4620, www.jutanegril.com. JUTA can also arrange individual itineraries. Prices for the same tour do vary, and you can save money by booking directly with JUTA or with the Jamaica Tourist Board, rather than through your own tour operator.

H

HEALTH AND MEDICAL CARE

Hygiene standards are generally high in Jamaica, and the tap water is drinkable. Mosquitoes can be a problem, especially just after sunset, and cases of Chikungunya virus passed by mosquitos have been confirmed on the island, so cover up or apply insect repellent. Don't step on the spiny sea urchins as you snorkel or dive; the spines will embed themselves in your flesh and the sores can become infected. Go easy on the alcohol, especially in the sunshine, as this can lead to dehydration. Take time to build a tan to avoid sunburn and sunstroke; use a sunscreen with a sufficiently high SPF.

Most hotels have an arrangement with a local doctor who will be on-call for any problem. Each major town on the island has a hospital; however, the nearest hospital to Ocho Rios is at St Ann's Bay, and the closest to Negril is at Savanna-la-Mar.

Always take out comprehensive insurance when you travel to cover unforeseen health emergencies or accidents.

L

LANGUAGE

English is the official language of Jamaica and is spoken by everyone on the island. However, the local population also uses a Caribbean-English creole language, Patois, when speaking with each other. It originally developed when the Elizabethan English of the British colonists mixed with the West African languages spoken by the African slaves transported to the island. With subsequent additions of English, African, and Spanish vocabulary, Jamaican English has evolved into an everyday medium that is difficult for outsiders to understand.

LGBTQ TRAVELLERS

In Jamaica, male homosexuality is an offence, with certain 'homosexual acts' punishable by prison. Consequently, homophobia is rife and there is no open gay scene, though LGBTQ rights are now one of the major political issues in the country. If you want to know more, have a look at J-Flag (Jamaica Forum for Lesbians, All-Sexuals and Gays; www.jflag.org), the largests LGBTQ rights organisation in Jamaica.

M

MEDIA

Radio and television. Jamaica has three TV nationwide stations and lots of local and cable channels. It has over a dozen radio stations, some of which are owned by the government. There are also a number of independent local radio stations and some online stations. Most hotels and many bars also receive satellite services, so you'll find BBC World, CNN and ESPN widely available.

Newspapers and magazines. The major national newspapers in Jamaica are the *Daily Gleaner* and *Sunday Gleaner* (http://jamaica-gleaner.com) and the *Jamaica Observer* (www.jamaicaobserver.com), alongside *The Star* (http://jamaica-star.com), an evening paper.

MONEY

Currency. The currency of Jamaica is the Jamaican dollar (J$; colloquially called the 'jay'), and there are 100 cents in each dollar. Paper bills are issued in denominations of $50, $100, $500, $1,000 and $5,000; coins are issued in denominations of 1 cent, 10 cents, 25 cents, 50 cents, $1, $5, $10 and $20. The smaller coins, being practically worthless, are being phased out. The US dollar is also widely accepted in shops and restaurants.

Jamaican dollars may be converted to foreign currency at the airport before departure upon presentation of an official exchange receipt. For visitors there are no restrictions on the import or export of foreign currencies, as long as they are declared, but the import or export of local currency is prohibited.

Travellers' cheques and credit cards. Travellers' cheques are generally widely accepted in Jamaica for cash in banks, for goods in shops, and for hotel and restaurant charges. Credit cards are also widely accepted except for fuel purchases, which must be made with cash (Jamaican or US dollars). If you want to obtain a cash advance with a credit card, you must take your card into a bank and produce photo ID. There are lots of ATMs (cash machines) in Jamaica, accepting a variety of international credit and debit cards.

Currency exchange. Money is changed at hotels, though at a less advantageous rate than in banks. There are also a number of 'Cambio' shops which are official money changers. You must have one official exchange receipt if you want to change money back before you return home. Changing money on the black market is illegal, but it is one of the services offered by street merchants. Beware of being cheated if you decide to use these unofficial money changers.

O

OPENING TIMES

Banks: 9am–2pm Monday to Thursday; 9am–4pm Friday.

Government offices (including Tourist Board): 8.30am–5pm, Monday to Thursday, 8.30am–4pm Friday.

Shops: 8.30am–4.30 or 5pm Monday to Friday, 8am–4pm Saturday, but this can vary enormously in resort towns and from low to high season.

P

POLICE

Police officers wear navy uniforms with red stripes on their hats and trousers. The emergency phone number for the police is **119**. The Jamaica Constabulary Force is based at 101–103 Old Hope Road, Kingston 6. For a list of local police stations visit www.jcf.gov.jm.

POST OFFICES

All major towns in Jamaica have a Post Office. These are open 8am–5pm Monday to Friday. However, the postal system is notoriously slow, so bear in mind that postcards often take three weeks to reach their destination. Post boxes are red, but unreliable. If you have anything particularly important or urgent to send, it is best to use a commercial carrier.

PUBLIC HOLIDAYS

Government offices and services are generally closed on the following days:

New Year's Day 1 January
Ash Wednesday
Good Friday
Easter Monday
Labour Day 23 May
Emancipation Day 1 August
Independence Day 6 August
National Heroes Day third Monday in October
Christmas Day 25 December
Boxing Day 26 December

R

RELIGION

Jamaica is a Christian island, with Protestant denominations in the majority. However, many other major religions are also represented and have places of worship. You will find that Jamaicans always dress very smartly to go to church. One of the significant minorities is the Rastafari movement, a way of life rather than a religion, whose true adherents are said to number fewer than 100,000. With their characteristic dreadlocked hair, they are seen as being almost synonymous with the image of Jamaica. Their influence on the popular culture of the island remains strong.

T

TELEPHONES

When calling from abroad, the country code for Jamaica is 876. When making an international call from Jamaica, always dial 00 before the country code. When in Jamaica, you need dial only the seven-digit local number; there are no area codes within Jamaica.

You can rent or buy mobile/cell phones, or buy a local SIM card to put in your own phone, but check that it is unlocked. Check with your home service provider that your phone will work in Jamaica, most will. Also check on your smartphone's connectivity, plus the use of apps, or Skype on a smartphone. Most of these options should work with the right phone. If you can access Wi-fi, check out internet phone services. Jamaican service providers are Flow (www.discoverflow.co/jamaica/) and Digicel (www.digiceljamaica.com).

TIME ZONES

Jamaica operates on Eastern Standard Time, which is 5 hours behind GMT; however, it does not switch to daylight saving time. The following chart shows the time in various cities in winter:

Los Angeles	New York	**Jamaica**	London	Sydney
9am	noon	**noon**	5pm	3am (next day)

TIPPING

Tipping is standard practice throughout the island, except at a few all-inclusive resorts where the 'no tipping' policy is clearly stated. It is common for a service charge to be automatically added to restaurant bills; this should be clearly stated on the menu or on the bill. If not, then a 10 percent to 15 percent tip should be added.

For taxi drivers, tip 10 percent to 15 percent; for porters, J$100–175 per bag; for hotel maids, J$100–175 per day.

TOURIST INFORMATION

For useful information to help you plan your trip, the Jamaica Tourist Board (www.visitjamaica.com) has offices in the following countries:

US: 5201 Blue Lagoon Drive, Suite 670, Miami, FL 33126 tel: (305) 665-0557; 1-800-526-2422 (toll-free); email: info@visitjamaica-usa.com.
UK: 1–2 Prince Consort Road, London SW7 2BZ, England, tel: (020) 7225-9090; email: mail@visitjamaica.uk.com.
Canada: 303 Eglinton Avenue East, Suite 200, Toronto, Ontario M4P 1L3, tel: (416) 482-7850, 1-800-465-2624 (toll free); email: jtb@visitjamaica-ca.com.

Tourist Offices can be found in the following locations:
Kingston: 64 Knutsford Boulevard, Kingston 5, tel: 929-9200; email: info@visitjamaica.com.
Montego Bay: Tourism Centre, Montego Bay Convention Centre, Rose Hall, St James, Montego Bay, tel: 952-4425.

TRANSPORT

The metropolitan areas of Kingston and Montego Bay both have decent bus systems. Taxis and bus franchises also provide easy commuting to coastal and interior areas of the island.

The tour company JUTA (see page 124) operates commercial air-conditioned bus services between the airports and the major resort areas. As an example, a one-way trip from Sangster Airport at Montego Bay to Negril costs around US$40 to Negril Beach and US$50 to West End. A private transfer costs around US$100 for 2 passengers.

Once you are settled, many restaurants and bars will provide free transportation in the evenings if you eat with them; just give them a call from your hotel.

Taxis are plentiful, but remember to only use the ones that have red number plates: these are registered and properly insured. Always agree on a price for the journey before you get into the taxi, as they do not carry meters. It is also a good idea to find out from other travellers what the going rate is for the journey that you want to make.

V

VISAS AND ENTRY REQUIREMENTS

Residents of the US and most Commonwealth and European countries do not need a visa to visit Jamaica, but must carry a passport valid for at least six months and a return ticket. Visitors from Canada can enter with a valid passport, naturalisation certificate, or photo ID with birth certificate, but a passport is essential to transit the US.

You should declare any unusual or expensive items (such as cameras or electrical goods) on arrival to assure the authorities that they are for personal use only.

W

WEBSITES AND INTERNET ACCESS

A number of websites can provide you with information about Jamaica before you book your trip, including details about hotels and attractions, car rental companies, and general facts and history:
www.visitjamaica.com – official site of the Jamaica Tourist Board
www.go-jamaica.com.

All these sites will link you with other useful sites for your trip. Jamaica has clusters of internet cafés, which are widely available in the tourist areas. Many of the larger hotels also offer the use of a computer in a public area or Wi-fi internet access for visitors with their own mobile device. You could also get a local sim card with mobile data when you arrive on the island.

Y

YOUTH HOSTELS

There are no youth hostels in Jamaica which are members of the Hostelling International Organisation. Several places call themselves hostels, but are really budget hotels. See www.hosteljamaica.com.

RECOMMENDED HOTELS

In both style and price, there is a wide choice of accommodation in Jamaica. At the upper end of the scale are the large, expensive luxury resorts and boutique hotels offering exclusivity, which are popular with honeymooners and celebrities. There is also a range of standard hotels at all levels. More modest accommodation can be found in small guesthouses and family-run hotels that offer clean rooms but few other facilities. A few historic plantation houses have been converted into hotels for a 'colonial feel'. Whatever your budget and taste, there will be something on the island to suit you.

Jamaica pioneered the all-inclusive hotel, where all your meals, drinks, sporting activities and other services are included in the price. This is the bedrock of mass market tourism on the island. Most of the resorts are in the north coast beach areas of Negril, Montego Bay and Ocho Rios. Some specialise in family holidays, others are for couples only. The resort chains have locations across the island, check their websites for details: Couples, www.couples.com; Decameron, www.decameron.com; Iberostar, www.iberostar.com; Riu, www.riu.com; Sandals, www.sandals.com; Sunset Resorts, www.sunsetresort.com; SuperClubs, www.superclubs.com.

The following selection of hotels covers a variety of accommodation options. The categories below indicate prices in US dollars per room, based on double occupancy.

$$$$	**over $200**
$$$	**$150–200**
$$	**$100–150**
$	**under $100**

MONTEGO BAY

Zoetry $$$$ *Little River, Ironshore (8km/5 miles east of Montego Bay at Mahoe Bay), tel: 1-888-496-3879),* www.zoetryresorts.com. Previously known as Coyaba Beach Resort, this family-owned hotel has 49 suites, all with balconies or terraces with either garden or sea view (a few suites have private swim-out pools). The hotel offers private fishing and diving charters, complimentary sunset boat rides and plenty of water sports. Land-based activities include yoga, cooking and bracelet workshops, gym and massage. Three healthy à la carte restaurants, a full bar and a café.

Toby's Resort $$ *1 Kent Avenue, Montego Bay, tel: 952-4370*, www.tobyresorts.com. At the end of the 'Hip Strip', this small hotel is convenient for the airport, bars, restaurants and beaches, all within walking distance. The staff are helpful and friendly, the rooms are simple but clean and comfortable with a balcony. There's a good restaurant, bar and pool.

Half Moon $$$$ *Rose Hall, Montego Bay, tel: 953-2211*, www.halfmoon.com. Beautifully-landscaped gardens and a private bay giving the resort its name. Set in 160 hectares (400 acres) of grounds, with 33 villas, 152 suites and 45 rooms, the hotel has been a luxury destination since 1954. The resort has four restaurants, a variety of snack bars, a spa and a shopping village. Land and water sports facilities include squash, tennis, health and fitness centre, equestrian centre and a par-72 championship golf course.

Ridgeway Guest House $ *34 Queen's Drive, Montego Bay, tel: 952-2709*, www.ridgewayguesthouse.com. A small, family-run inn with 10 simple rooms in a modern block, built in the garden of the original guest house and within walking distance of the airport. The staff are friendly and can help to arrange excursions, car hire is available on site. Good value accommodation.

Round Hill Hotel and Villas $$$$ *John Pringle Drive, Montego Bay, tel: 956-7050, 800-972-2159*, www.roundhill.com. A casually elegant hotel set in a former pineapple plantation at the edge of the crystal clear waters of a private white-sand beach. There is a lovely infinity pool, water sports centre with some complimentary activities, diving, deep-sea fishing and yachting can be arranged, tennis with resident pro, spa with fitness centre, jogging/walking path, boutique and shop, free shuttle to main shops. 36 ocean-front rooms designed by Ralph Lauren and 27 individually owned villas with 2–5 bedrooms. The cuisine is international with Jamaican touches.

The Tryall Club $$$$ *20km (12 miles) west of Montego Bay, tel: 956-5660, 800-238-5290 (toll-free from US)*, www.tryallclub.com. A luxurious seaside villa hideaway with a championship golf course on a 890-hectare (2,200-acre) tropical estate, originally a sugar plantation until 1918 when coconut palms were planted. Presided over by a Georgian Great House and situated in manicured gardens and rolling hills, with 2.5km (11/2 miles) of coastline and a palm-dotted white sand beach. Privately-owned villas with 2–8 bedrooms.

Wexford $$–$$$ *39 Gloucester Avenue, Montego Bay, tel: 952-2854*, www.thewexfordhotel.com. Convenient for nightlife and the 'Hip Strip', just across the road from the public beach. 60 rooms and one-bedroom apartments, sea view or garden view overlooking the pool. Tiled floors, air conditioning, TV, phone, balconies – a good option if you want to be in town. Shuttle service and free entry to Aquasol Beach. Dine at *Rosella's* for Jamaican cuisine.

RUNAWAY BAY

Club Ambiance $$$ *Main Road, St Ann, Runaway Bay, tel: 973-4605*, www.clubambiance.com. Large all-inclusive resort with 100 rooms in five blocks. All rooms have air conditioning and a sea view. There is also a refurbished three-bedroom, private beachfront villa available to rent. Three beaches (one is clothes optional). Nightclub and restaurant on the complex. No guests under 18 years old.

Piper's Cove Resort $–$$ *Salem, Runaway Bay, tel: 973-7156*, www.piperscoveresortjamaica.com. 14 one-bedroom apartments, some with sea view, and six studio apartments with kitchenette, bathroom, private balcony, safety-deposit box, cable TV, air-conditioning. There are pleasant gardens and it is popular for weddings. It has a private beach, pool, restaurant and games room.

OCHO RIOS AND ENVIRONS

Goldeneye $$$$ *Oracabessa, St Mary, tel: 6229-007, 800-688-7678* www.goldeneye.com. An exclusive and luxurious retreat created around the former home of James Bond author, Ian Fleming. The resort, which is part of the Island Outpost boutique hotel chain, has 11 beach or lagoon cottages including the Ian Fleming villa, secluded in lush gardens with private coves and beaches. Modern decor, with state-of-the-art amenities. All have access to the *James Bond Beach Club*, with three beaches, a two-storey, open-air restaurant and water sports.

Hibiscus Lodge $$–$$$ *83–87 Main Street, Ocho Rios, tel: 974-2676.* Rooms perched on top of cliffs surrounded by gardens, with paths and stairways down to the sea, but no beach. The reef just offshore is good for snorkelling. Located a short way out of the centre of Ocho Rios, but within walking distance of the shops and nightlife. The hotel has a good restaurant on site and a bar overlooking the water. Good-sized swimming pool and cliff-top Jacuzzi, 26 simple rooms with air conditioning and fans, balconies have a sea view; you pay for the pretty setting rather than the amenities, but good value for Ocho Rios.

Jamaica Inn $$$$ *Main Street, Ocho Rios, tel: 441-2044* www.jamaicainn.com. This has been one of the island's best hotels since the 1950s, with 47 suites in pretty gardens overlooking a lovely, private beach. The award-winning hotel offers excellent amenities and personal service; it is beautifully designed and maintained. Luxury facilities include spa treatments and delicious gourmet local cuisine.

Rooms on the Beach $$ *Main Street, Ocho Rios, tel: 1-877-467-8737,* www.roomsresorts.com. A budget option from the SuperClubs chain, with 99 air-conditioned rooms in a three-storey beachfront block near the centre of Ocho Rios. Facilities include kayaking, windsurfing, snorkelling and scuba diving, and there is a pool on the property and free Wi-fi. Four meal plans to choose from. There is also a branch in Negril.

Sandals Royal Plantation $$$$ *Main Street, Ocho Rios, tel: 888-726-3257, in the UK tel: 0800-022-3030, 207-582-9895,* www.sandals.co.uk.

Seafront resort in operation since the 1950s, with 74 ocean view suites and one exclusive villa, three gourmet restaurants, spa, water sports, scuba diving and little luxuries such as 24-hour room service, beach butler and afternoon tea on the terrace. Bedrooms have mahogany beds with comfortable down mattresses and Italian sheets. Guests also have access to the Sandals Golf and Country Club, with complimentary green fees and transport to and from the 18-hole championship course.

PORT ANTONIO AND THE EAST

Great Huts $–$$$$ *Boston Bay, tel: 993-8888; 353-3388*, www.greathuts.com. Located on the cliffs of Boston Bay this seafront eco-resort is perfect for a romantic weekend or a holiday with the whole family. Accommodation is in rustic African-style bamboo huts, treehouses and tents furnished with exotic textiles, paintings and carvings, and comfortable bamboo and driftwood beds. Some units have hot water, some share bathrooms and all have electricity. Surfing, snorkelling and yoga facilities. The price includes breakfast and there is a restaurant on the property. The Boston Jerk Centre is nearby.

Frenchman's Cove Bed & Breakfast $–$$$$ *Frenchman's Cove, Portland, tel: 993-7270, 564-9779*, www.frenchmanscove.com. In a beautiful location on an 18-hectare (45-acre) private estate outside Port Antonio, with a white sand beach and freshwater stream. Simply decorated villas of varying sizes nestled on the cliff sides, or rooms and suites in the main house. This long-established resort is slightly dated but quiet and relaxing. Facilities include a beachfront grill-style restaurant and two bars.

Goblin Hill Villas at San San $$$–$$$$ *San San, tel: 933-7443, 630-1540*, www.goblinhill.com. A lush site set high on a hillside with excellent views over the sea. Self-contained villas of one or two bedrooms with fully equipped kitchens staffed with cook/housekeeper. Freshwater swimming pool and two tennis courts. Complimentary access to Frenchman's Cove; nature trails lead through the gardens with extensive lawns and woods.

Jamaica Palace Hotel $$$–$$$$ *Williamsfield, tel: 993-7721, 712-4062, 993-7731*, www.jamaica-palacehotel.com. Large comfortable hotel with

80 suites and rooms with round beds, colourful floral furnishings, air conditioning and bath/shower. Also on the property are an art gallery, a swimming pool and a good restaurant.

Mocking Bird Hill Hotel $$$–$$$$ *Port Antonio, tel: 993-7267*, www.hotelmockingbirdhill.com. On a hilltop above the town, five minutes' drive from Frenchman's Cove beach. A tranquil hideaway nestled in the verdant foothills of the Blue Mountains, decorated throughout with original art and with an art gallery attached. The hotel promotes environmental awareness, encouraging sustainable development and is popular with birdwatchers. Fine restaurant, serving nouvelle Caribbean cuisine. Ten white-tiled rooms, with Jamaican hand-crafted bamboo furniture and locally-printed fabrics, offer a garden view downstairs; superior rooms upstairs with views of the hillside and the sea beyond.

Strawberry Fields Together! $–$$$$ *Robin's Bay, St Mary, tel: 436-6395, in the UK tel: 203-3183-784*, www.strawberryfieldstogether.com. Secluded and rustic standard or deluxe cottages sleep 25 dorm-style or 7 couples. There is also a camping area where you can pitch your tent for $15 per night per person. Quiet during the week but busy at weekends with Jamaican families staying over or just here for the day. Private beach with life guard, snorkelling, volleyball, trampoline, table tennis and organised excursions. Large nature reserve. Meal plans available; local cuisine.

Trident Hotel $$$$ *Anchovy, Port Antonio, tel: 633-7100, 1-800-300-6220;* www.tridentportantonio.com. Luxurious sophistication on the northeast shore. Thirteen glamorous oceanfront villas with modernist interior, terrace, private pool, and broadband internet access. Located on site, *Mike's Supper Club* is a smart music and dining venue where you can revel in both jazz and Japanese-Jamaican cuisine. The resort amenities also include a private beach, gym and spa.

THE BLUE MOUNTAINS

Forres Park Guest House $–$$$$ *Mavis Bank, tel: 927-8275*, www.forrespark.com. Entrance on the main road by the Mavis Bank Coffee Factory, rooms are available in the Swiss chalet-style main house or in nearby cosy cabins on the working coffee farm. Trails for hiking and birdwatching, although most of the birds can be seen at daybreak from the balcony. Guides can be arranged for a trip to Blue Mountain Peak. Customised spa treatments will rejuvenate you after your excursions.

Lime Tree Farm $$$$ *Tower Hill, Mavis Bank, tel: 446-0230;* www.limetreefarm.com. Four cottages on a working coffee farm with views of the Blue Mountains and surrounding valleys. Large bedrooms, bathroom and terrace, spacious enough for a small family. Price includes transfers from Kingston and all meals with a bottle of wine at dinner. Delicious food using local ingredients and herbs. Good hiking and birdwatching.

KINGSTON AREA

Courtleigh Hotel and Suites $$$–$$$$ *85 Knutsford Boulevard, Kingston 5, tel: 936-3570*, www.courtleigh.com. In the financial district of New Kingston, convenient for shopping and eating. Rooms have tea/coffee maker, air conditioning, Wi-fi, dataport, cable TV, hairdryer, with an outdoor swimming pool and fitness room, restaurant and bar.

Grand Port Royal Hotel $$$–$$$$ *Port Royal, tel: 967-8494*, www.grandportroyal.com. Situated in Port Royal at the entrance to Kingston Harbour, this hotel offers commanding views of the city skyline and the Blue Mountains. Spacious accommodation in 60 rooms and suites. Facilities include a freshwater swimming pool, gaming lounge, pub and two restaurants, including the acclaimed restaurant next to the marina, which is lovely at night

Indies Hotel $ *5 Holborn Road, Kingston 10, tel: 926-2952*, www.indieshotel.com. 15 rather small rooms in two wings overlooking a patio garden. Single, double and triple rooms available, all with bathroom, air conditioning, cable TV and phone. Simple but adequate with good, budget restaurant and bar. Convenient for shops, restaurants, entertainment and sightseeing.

The Jamaica Pegasus $$$$ *81 Knutsford Boulevard, Kingston 5, tel: 926-3691*, www.jamaicapegasus.com. Situated in the financial and business district, close to many of the area's foremost attractions. All 300 rooms and suites are equipped with high-speed internet access, satellite TV, hair dryers, safes, complimentary coffee- and tea-making facilities, and balconies with either mountain or pool/ocean view. Non-smoking floors. Restaurants and cafés offer a variety of fare, plus there are bars and evening entertainment.

Strawberry Hill Hotel $$$$ *New Castle Road, Irish Town, St Andrew, tel: 944-8400*, (800) 232-4972, www.strawberryhillhotel.com. Romantic, delightful cottages feature traditional 19th-century Jamaican architecture for an authentic atmosphere. Near Kingston and surrounded by the Blue Mountains and extensive gardens, with exceptional panoramic views (including Kingston) and an infinity pool, small but perfect. Excellent fusion cuisine. Spa treatments, yoga pavilion, plunge pool and sauna encourage health and well-being. The hotel, part of the Island Outpost chain, has won many awards for its architecture and design, and is one of the best places to stay in the whole of the Caribbean.

TREASURE BEACH (SOUTH COAST)

Ital-Rest Cottages $ *Treasure Beach, tel: 421-8909*. Two simple, rustic, thatched cottages with a mountain or sea view, each with two bedrooms, bathroom and kitchen. The café in the garden has vegan and vegetarian food, music, dominoes and table tennis. Local restaurant close by. Friendly and helpful, 100m/yds to the sea, this is genuine laid-back Jamaica.

Jakes $–$$$$ *Calabash Bay, Treasure Beach, tel: 965-3000*, www.jakeshotel.com. An eclectic collection of colourful cottages set atop low cliffs in a secluded bay, and a truly special place to stay. Created by painter-photographer-art director Sally Henzell and part of the Island Outpost chain. Each room has a different theme, from Jamaican shack to Mexican pueblo and they vary in size from a single room with a garden view to a 4-bedroom cottage, including delightful, romantic honeymoon suites. All have in-room music equipment and free use of the hotel's extensive music collection. Tropical ceiling fans and mosquito nets maintain the traditional feel. Rooms also in the Henzell's historic home. Two excellent restaurants with the freshest of seafood and other local specialities. Media room with Wi-fi and computer for guests' use, spa and yoga retreats. Swim at Jack Sprat Beach or in the seawater swimming pool.

Sunset Resort $–$$$$ *Calabash Bay, Treasure Beach, St Elizabeth, tel: 965-0143,* www.sunsetresort.com. 14 rooms and suites overlook Calabash bay and beach where there are fishing boats pulled up on the sand. American and Jamaican-owned, it is good for family groups as suites can become apartments, and large parties can rent the entire villa. Staff can arrange deep-sea fishing in traditional boats or motor cruisers. Rather odd astro turf around the pool. Satellite TV, air conditioning, coffee makers, flowery wall decorations, restaurant and lounge.

NEGRIL

The Caves $$$$ *One Love Drive, Negril, tel: 957-0270,* www.islandoutpost.com. Part of the Island Outpost hotel chain, this award-winning romantic hotel is perched on the cliffs above the sea. Luxury cottages of thatched wood and stone. Inside the caves are an intimate dining room and part of the spa. Steps lead down to the water where you can snorkel in more caves. Relax with a yoga class or explore the area on bicycles, kayaks or rafts. Several dining options and the *Blackwell Rum Bar*. No children under 16.

Charela Inn $$–$$$$ *Norman Manley Boulevard, Negril, tel: 957-4648,* www.charela.com. Rooms on the beach in a long-established, family-run hotel with Jamaican-French owners and French chef, so food is a priority. There is a bakery in the hotel and they have one of the best wine lists on the island. Rooms vary in size and amenities but are well-equipped and three are adapted for wheelchair users.

Rockhouse Hotel $$–$$$ *West End, Negril, tel: 807-0868, 957-4373,* www.rockhousehotel.com. Commanding a rocky promontory in West

End with views of spectacular sunsets, this collection of thatch-roofed villas has a tranquil setting. Cliff-top pool, spa and access to swimming and snorkelling in Pristine Cove more than make up for the lack of a sandy beach. Not suitable for children under 12. 34 rooms, studios and villas.

Seasplash Resort $$–$$$$ *Norman Manley Boulevard, tel: 957-4041*, in the UK tel 0800-7297-2900, www.seasplash.com. On the narrow part of Negril's 11-km (7-mile) sandy beach, within walking distance of beach bars and restaurants. Rooms and suites are spacious and comfortable, with good fittings and furnishings, all well-equipped. Low-season prices drop by one-third from high-season rates and are excellent value. Very good restaurant on site, *Norma's* (see page 113), with steps down to the sea.

Tensing Pen $$$–$$$$ *West End, Negril, tel: 957-0387*, http://tensingpen.com. 16 luxurious rooms in cottages perched on cliffs with hammocks and lots of private areas for quiet sunbathing and relaxation around the property. Laidback, unpretentious and sociable. Yoga and massage facilities on site, lots of activities offered. Breakfast is included and dinner is served daily using fresh local produce.

Xtabi Resort $–$$$$ *Lighthouse Road, West End, Negril, tel: 957-0121*, www.xtabinegril.com. Seafront, poolside or garden cottages, rooms or a suite, on the cliffs offer a choice of simple or luxury accommodation, all with balcony or veranda, some with air conditioning. Steps lead down to caves for snorkelling. Native wood floors and rustic furnishings, outside showers with privacy walls. All rooms have safes, some have kitchenettes and many have refrigerators; the garden rooms are more modern, with tiled floors and air-conditioning. Cliffside bar and restaurant.

INDEX

Accommodation 115, 132
Accompong 39
airports 115
Alligator Hole 78
Alligator Pond 78
Annotto Bay 47
Appleton Distillery 74

Bamboo Avenue 75
Barnett Estate 32
Belvedere Estate 33
bicycle rental 116
Black River 76
Bluefields 83
Blue Lagoon 57
Blue Mountain Peak 60
Blue Mountains 60
  coffee plantations 62
Blue Mountains and John Crow National Park 61
boat charters 88
Bob Marley Mausoleum 41
Bogle, Paul 60
Boston Bay 57
Brimmer Hall Plantation 48

Car hire 118
Castleton Botanical Gardens 49
Central Highlands 72
children 98
climate 119
clothing 120
Cockpit Country 38
coffee plantations 62
Columbus Park 40
Cornwall Barracks 58
cricket 92
crime and safety 120
cycling 91

Discovery Bay 39
diving 88
driving 121
Dunn's River Falls 45

Electricity 122
embassies 122

Falmouth 36
Falmouth Swamp Safari 36
Fern Gully 46
festivals 99
Firefly 47
Fort Charles 69
Fort Charles Maritime Museum 70
Frenchman's Cove 56

Galina Point 47
Ganja Planes 41
Giddy House (Port Royal) 70
Goldeneye 48
golf 89
Great Morass 82
Great Morass Mangrove Swamp 76
Green Grotto Caves 40
Greenwood Great House 35
guides and tours 124

Health and medical care 125
Hellshire Hills 73
Holland Bay 59
horse racing 92
horse riding 91

James Bond Beach Club 48

Kingston 63
  Bob Marley Museum 68
  Devon House 67
  Emancipation Park 67
  Gordon House 66
  Headquarters House 65
  Institute of Jamaica 66
  Jamaica Conference Centre 65
  Jamaica House 68
  King's House 68
  National Gallery 65
  National Heroes Park 66
  National Library 66
  Natural History Museum 66
  Parade 67
  Vale Royal 68
  William Grant Park 66

Lime Cay (Port Royal) 50, 70
Little London 83
Long Bay (East) 50, 58
Long Bay (Negril) 50, 80

Mammee Bay 59
Mangrove Alley 77
Mannings School 83
Maroons 58

Martha Brae River 37
media 125
money 126
Montego Bay 28
  Aquasol Theme Park 31
  Cage 29
  Cornwall Beach 31
  Doctor's Cave Beach 31, 50
  Fort Montego 30
  Fort Montego Craft Park 30
  Gloucester Avenue 30
  Harbour Street Craft Market 30
  Montego Bay Freeport 31
  Montego Bay Marine Park 32
  Montego Bay Yacht Club 31
  Pier 1 32
  Ring 30
  Sam Sharpe Square 29
  Walter Fletcher Beach 31
Moore Town 58
Morant Bay 60
Morant Point Lighthouse 59

National Archaeological and Historical Museum 70
Navy Island 53
Negril 79
  Anancy Village 80
  Booby Cay 50, 80
  Kool Runnings Water Park 80
  Long Bay 50, 80
  Negril Lighthouse 82
  Rick's Café 81
  West End 81
nightlife 93
Nine Mile 41

Ocho Rios 42
  Ocho Rios Fort 43
  Turtle Beach 43
Oracabessa 47
Oyster Bay 38

Palisadoes 69
Paradise Park 83
police 127
Port Antonio 51
  Bonnie View Hotel 54
  Hill, The 54
  St George's Village 54
Port Morant 59
Port Royal 69
Prospect Plantation 46

Rafting 37, 55
Reach Falls 59
Rio Grande 54
Rocklands Bird Sanctuary 33
Rose Hall Great House 34
Royal Palm Reserve 82
Runaway Bay 40
  Canyon 41
  Ricky's Reef 40

San San 57
Savanna-la-Mar 83
Sharpe, Samuel 29
Shaw Park Botanical Gardens 44
shopping 94
snorkelling 86
Spanish Town 72
  Jamaica Archives and Records Office 72
  Jamaican People's Museum of Craft and Technology 73
  Old King's House 73
  Parade 72
  Rodney Memorial 72
St Ann's Bay 41

Telephones 128
time zones 129
transport 130
Treasure Beach 50, 77
Tryall Estate 79

Visas 131

Walking 90
White River 46
White River Valley 46

YS Falls 76

Berlitz pocket guide

JAMAICA

Ninth Edition 2019

Editor: Tatiana Wilde
Author: Jack Altman
Head of DTP and Pre-Press: Rebeka Davies
Managing Editor: Carine Tracanelli
Picture Editor: Tom Smyth
Cartography Update: Carte
Update Production: Apa Digital
Photography Credits: Alamy 59, 92; Public Domain 17, 21, 22; Chukka Caribbean Adventures 91; Getty Images 4TC, 65, 75, 84; Greenwood Great House 35; iStock 39, 44, 61, 63, 81, 103; Jamaica Tourist Board 7R, 37, 40, 67, 94; Kevin Cummins/Apa Publications 4ML, 4TL, 5TL, 5TR, 5ML, 5MR, 5BR, 7L, 11, 12, 24, 28, 30, 31, 33, 34, 43, 45, 47, 49, 51, 52, 53, 54, 56, 57, 68, 71, 73, 77, 78, 82, 88, 90, 93, 96, 98, 101, 104, 106, 107; Michael Runkel 6L; Pete Bennett 15, 19, 32, 86; Photoshot 4MC; Shutterstock 1, 6R, 26, 55
Cover Picture: Getty Images

Distribution
UK, Ireland and Europe: Apa Publications (UK) Ltd; sales@insightguides.com
United States and Canada: Ingram Publisher Services; ips@ingramcontent.com
Australia and New Zealand: Woodslane; info@woodslane.com.au
Southeast Asia: Apa Publications (SN) Pte; singaporeoffice@insightguides.com
Worldwide: Apa Publications (UK) Ltd; sales@insightguides.com

Special Sales, Content Licensing and CoPublishing
Insight Guides can be purchased in bulk quantities at discounted prices. We can create special editions, personalised jackets and corporate imprints tailored to your needs. sales@insightguides.com; www.insightguides.biz

Printed in China by CTPS

Contact us
Every effort has been made to provide accurate information in this publication, but changes are inevitable. The publisher cannot be responsible for any resulting loss, inconvenience or injury. We would appreciate it if readers would call our attention to any errors or outdated information. We also welcome your suggestions; please contact us at: berlitz@apaguide.co.uk
www.insightguides.com/berlitz